LAUGHTER AND LIES AROUND THE POTBELLIED STOVE

(O.B. Gay's Country Store Legacy)

BRENDA MARTIN GAY

Scott,

Hope you enjoy,

Brenda Gay

Dec 2017

Keep Traveling &
Keep Writing !!!

919-914-1591
bmartingay@gmail.com

Laughter and Lies around the Potbellied Stove Copyright © 2017 by Brenda Gay. All rights reserved.

ISBN-13:
978-1546461012

ISBN-10:
1546461019

Paperbacks printed by CreateSpace Independent Publishing Platform, Charleston, SC: Available from Amazon.com and other retail outlets.

DEDICATION

This book is dedicated to my parents, Oris B. and Ruby M. Gay, who personified the relentless determination to follow their dreams and persevere amid the countless obstacles that threatened their happiness and success.

Filled with love and admiration for my wonderful parents, I am honored for the privilege to capture exerts from their colorful life experiences. I will forever be grateful for the many blessings I derived from their rural store setting.

Without these two amazing people, this book would never have materialized. Thus, this special dedication is made to Daddy and Mother with my deepest gratitude.

RECOGNITION

To the late Jerri Cox Bilodeau, my very dear friend of 33 years, who passed away September 13, 2016. Jerri spent countless hours doing computer research for me to assure I was using accurate dates or descriptions associated with old vehicles, historical events, and item identifications. Her committed effort to assist with what she perceived to be my success in completing this book was an inspiration. Thank you, "Toot!"

To the late Trey Martin, my special cousin of 65 years and my favorite traveling and photographing sidekick, who passed away October 28, 2016. Trey is responsible for so many of the actual pictures of the store, for continuous downloading pictures on the computer and for making sure there were enough backups preserved with each new information added throughout the writing of the book. He also drove me around to cities, towns, and rural areas in attempts to interview others, take

photos, and gather more information for my writing. His enthusiasm was second only to mine as he anxiously awaited the finished product. Thank you, "favorite cuz!"

ACKNOWLEDGMENTS

To my talented and insightful editor, ASHLEIGH CAROLINE BILODEAU, whom I affectionately refer to as "my granddaughter," I owe a debt of gratitude for the countless hours she spent reading my writes and rewrites (and there were many.) Her command of English grammar, reviewing and rephrasing words were skills she learned as editor of the Lyricist from Campbell University where she graduated magna cum laude in the spring of 2015. Because of her insightful suggestions and her relentless patience, my writing became less repetitive, words began to flow smoother, and clarity seemed to evolve. Her unceasing encouragement promoted my self-esteem and left me with an overwhelming desire to fill the pages of my book with a wide variation of memorable events.

To CHRISTAL LEIGH, also affectionately known as "my granddaughter," many thanks for the "You can do it Granny!" comebacks when I became discouraged and impatient with my writing endeavor. She reminded me repeatedly that quitting was not an option! Taking a small break and watching that full-of-energy, eighth-grader perform her singing videos, I had a renewed sense of ambition and was ready to write again.

 To my cousin, ANGIE PARTIN, a world of thanks for providing a lap top on which I could do research, store interview notes, do countless writes and rewrites. Replacing my old, outdated desk top computer with the lap top enabled me to compile and complete this book faster. With the added benefit of being able to transport information from one physical location to another, I was afforded the opportunity to grasp and immediately record ideas and memories when and where they appeared.

Last but certainly not least, I extend my sincere appreciation to those who shared information or provided photos of their friends and family members to be included in this book. I hope you will be pleased with the way they were portrayed herein. It has been a pleasure to reminisce about those individuals who constituted a picture of wholesome rural living and entertainment.

Thank you:

Adrian Murray, Jr., Alice Whitley Taylor, Alvin Wright, Becky Jo Saunders, Bettie Phillips Parrish, Bonnie Murray Perry, C.A. Lloyd, Cordell Richards, Curtis Alford, Dale Gay Perry David Earl Baker, Donna Baker, Doris Duke Champion, Franklin Barham, Gene & Yvonne Lloyd, Ginger Gay Caldwell, Henry Bunn, Hilda Gay, Janice Perry Strickland, Jimmy C. Pearce, Johnny Locklear, Josephine Perry Alford, Kim Martin Pace, Larry Blackley, Larry D. Perry, Larue Pearce Richards, Lester Roy Barham, Linda Rogers Jones, Lucille Baker Burchell, Lyn Richards Massey, Marie N. Gay, Pat Mitchell, Randy Privette, Ronnie V. Perry, Scott Johnston, Sylvia L. Richards, Thomas Pearce, Tina Bray, Tish Gay, Wayne & Linda Blackley.

Contents

PROLOGUE	i
PRELUDE	iii
HIS JOURNEY BEGINS	1
"RED BIRD"	3
NEW BUILDING CONSTRUCTED	5
"BUBBLE" GAS PUMP FILLING STATION	9
POST-DEPRESSION YEARS' SALES	11
POST-DEPRESSION YEARS' PROMOS	15
HE CUT THE CHEESE	21
DIVERSIFICATION, DETERMINATION, DEDICATION	25
OLD SALES SLIPS WEAVE PICTORIAL HISTORY	29
GATHER AROUND THE STOVE	31
HIDDEN AWAY QUIET AS A MOUSE	35
SHARED JOYS OF YOUNG ADULTHOOD	43
RERUNS & RECYCLES ABOUND	49
VOLUNTEERS TO THE RESCUE	53
A HAVEN FROM STORMS	63
VALUABLE IN-STORE EDUCATION	65
THE BAKERS DOZEN	71
Zollie Thomas Pearce	77
John "Eacho" Richards	79
Ronald "Lytchford" Gay, Sr.	81
Howard Marshall Phillips	85
Agerford Oliver Gay	87

Lewis Evans Lloyd	89
James Ruffin Whitley	91
Irey Leonard Gay	95
Aubrey Leonard Gay	97
Clarence Edward Duke, Sr.	101
Eddie "The Healer" Blackley	103
Hilary James Pearce	105
FAMILIAR SURNAMES AND NICKNAMES	107
NO NEED FOR COMPETITION	111
SOMETHING MUST BE BREWING	117
BEER & WINE SALES CONFLICT	119
SERENITY INTERRUPTED	123
DON'T MESS WITH HIM	133
INNOCENCE OF A CHILD	141
MONDAY MORNING MYSTERY	145
HIS JOURNEY ENDS	149

PROLOGUE

A Notation from the Author

The intended purpose for writing this book was not for notoriety. Rather, it was written to capture and share precious memories of a period when the "simple life" was the norm and people found comfort in that reality.

Come with me while I tread down memory lane in search of events that will present a heart-warming experience for you, the reader, to share. May you find pleasure as you witness the "never a dull moment" life of those individuals and events that unfolded and allowed this writing to materialize.

Retiring a few months prior to his 74th birthday, my daddy, Oris "O. B" Gay, realized his goal to complete fifty years in the country-store business.

I planned to write a book about his store experiences soon after the doors of the building were closed. Unfortunately, I never seemed to have enough time to expand my thoughts on the subject. Now it seems there is nothing but time; therefore, there are no more excuses for not writing this tribute to my parents and to those colorful patrons responsible for the lies and laughter around the old potbellied stove.

Completion of the writing of this book a few months after my own 74th birthday represents a successful goal attainment for me as well.

To all the literary artists out there, both skilled and unskilled, beginners and seasoned alike, I commend you for your persistent efforts to capture and record life's moments.

Obviously, I am a first-time-writer. When I embarked on this literary journey, I discovered a new admiration for all writers. The relentless number of hours engaged in research and the countless writes and rewrites presented me with an ever-increasing challenge. I found myself determined to overcome my limited verbal dexterity and, in the process, improved my organizational skills also. There was no room for doubt or discouragement. With the aid of my Webster's dictionary and spell check on my computer, I pressed on.

This endeavor has, at times, consumed my every waking hour. With each place I visited, and every word I read in newspapers, magazine articles and books, or heard on the radio or television, I found myself contemplating ways to implement new ideas into my writing project. A single word could start my mind's wheels turning and I would delve into another storyline.

Eating, resting, watching television, or even riding along the highway, I continuously paused and jotted down notes for future writings. My central thought system overloaded with new topics. At times, this obsession overwhelmed me. Before going to sleep some nights, I sat on the side of my bed, removed my pad and pencil from the night stand, and recorded another spur-of-the-moment thought. Material ideas sometimes penetrated my dream process; whereupon, I again sat on the bedside and recorded my latest thoughts before they became caught up in my dream and drifted away.

Never had I experienced such an increasing urgency to record a bit of factual history relative to growing up in Rural America. Time had come for someone to capture that shared sense of pride and passion derived from being reared among those individuals who represented the heart and soul of good old country living. Why shouldn't I be that someone?

PRELUDE

Riding through the streets of Rolesville, NC, my eyes focus upon an all too familiar building that sits on the back lot of the local flea market once owned and operated by Mr. Hubert Eddins. No longer is this building a permanent fixture on the corner of Hopkins Chapel Road and Halifax Road, located just prior to the Wake/Franklin County line near the intersection of Riley, North Carolina. Because of its upheaval and placement in virtual seclusion, this old building has lost its sense of vitality.

The walls are now empty and filled with gloominess. Shelves, once filled from floor to ceiling with a wide variety of merchandise, as illustrated in this photo of the Edsel Martin family, have been removed.

Spaciousness greets you and immediately you are surrounded by nothing but quietness. No longer are there sounds of yarn-swapping laughter and echoes of lies bouncing off the walls. The building remains soundless and an overwhelming feeling of loneliness echoes throughout.

Gone are the upright and chest-type drink cases filled with ice-laced cold beverages. The elongated bench placed in front of the shelves, the chairs with their twill-woven seats, the wooden nail kegs that were transformed into tall stools, and the trusty old pot-bellied stove with its long smoke stack have all been removed. Missing is the primitive, handmade wooden checkout counter along with its ten key, hand-crank adding machine and the non-electric metal cash register. Look closely at the floor and you will see the tell-tale signs of where candy cases with sliding glass doors occupied that space. Children and adults could freely open the sliding doors and fill their little brown paper bags with an assortment of sweets found on the glass shelves. Goodies such as Mary Jane, tootsie rolls, orange slices, pecan sticks, bits of honey, and fiery-red jaw breakers were just a few of the choices that could be purchased for only one cent each. Miraculously, neither the glass doors nor the glass shelves were ever broken even though they withstood countless hours of activity.

The only original structures that remain on this antique building are the steel bar-covered windows, the wide beams in the high structured ceiling, and the wooden floors now covered to conceal the bullet holes left by armed robbers in a 1949 holdup at the store. Tin still covers the building exterior and roof and access to the building remains through wooden doors both on the front and the rear of the store.

Accompanying me on a nostalgic walk through this old store, my granddaughter, Ashleigh, rendered a very descriptive prose of how she perceived the building.

"Metallic panels gilded with the garnet-colored rust of time, the old country store lives on."

"A frail skeleton devoid of callow giggles and boisterous reprimands, the weathered apparition clings to the ground of the living. The sharp tang of chewing tobacco has long faded from the dust…of the family-owned business."

Her perception reiterates the enveloping still of quietness and the stifling air of despair that is created therein. If these now silent walls could but only talk; oh, what an entwining tale they would weave. Reminiscing sounds of welcoming greetings would once again ring out. "Do drop in," "grab yourself a 'drank' and moon pie," "pull up a nail keg and set for a spell," and swap a few "loafer's Lodge" yarns around the old potbellied stove.

Join me as I attempt to recapture cultural, and sometimes comical, events that present this old country store business as a legend in time.

O.B. Gay's Store was in full operation six days a week from January 1, 1933 through December 31, 1983. This country store mercantile business persevered amid the depression-era challenges and made an impression on the history of our rural community and the lives of the people who frequented its premises.

The incidents presented in the following pages are written in appreciation of the countless hours my parents, Oris and Ruby Gay, accommodated their friends and neighbors as proprietors of their country store. Many times, after hearing a knock on the door in the middle of the night, my dad would comply with someone's request and return to the store to fill the empty gas tank of their car. Other times he would arise before the sun came up, go to the store, fill the old stove with either wood or coal, and have a warm fire waiting to greet the early rising hunters or the school children waiting for their bus. Neither of my parents ever complained about going the "extra mile" for their customers and friends.

    To show appreciation for my parents' dedication; and to recognize some of the people and events that inspired this writing endeavor, I proudly present to you, "Laughter and Lies around the Old Potbellied Stove."

Chapter One

HIS JOURNEY BEGINS

Two brothers, Leonard (25) and Oris (23), lived in their Franklin County home with their mama, Lillie Gay, and operated the farm for her following the death of their father, Ollie Gay, in 1930. They each shared the same desire to venture out on their own. Like so many families depending on farm income, the 1929 Wall Street stock market collapse resulted in falling crop prices and little money with which to survive. Commodity prices plunged and an onset of food and gas rationing emerged. Though they were far from destitute, times were hard and saving money was virtually impossible. Thus, the two brothers were reluctant to borrow any money to purchase property.

While visiting with Lillie during Christmas of 1932, Ollie's sister, Viola, engaged in a conversation about a decision she and husband, Redford, had made.

"Red and I are thinking about selling our land near the County Line. There are probably sixty or more acres in that tract. Do you think any of your boys would be interested in buying the land?"

Oris and Leonard were in the adjoining room and overheard the conversation. They were very interested in acquiring the land and immediately approached their aunt.

"Aunt Pink, were you serious about selling your land? We would love to buy some land and hopefully build our own homes."

Their aunt replied, "That would be wonderful. I would much rather sell that property to someone in the family, especially my nephews. I know my brother would be pleased to know you were building your own homes and raising your families on the wide, open stretches of land."

Amid this happy occasion, the brothers suddenly realized neither of them possessed the required funds to make this acquisition. With anticipation and some skepticism, they decided to approach their father's brother, Williford Gay, a neighboring homeowner and profitable farmer.

"Uncle Williford, we have the opportunity to buy some land of our own at a very reasonable price."

Williford had a strong suspicion these boys were approaching him for financial assistance. He felt they were creditable and would honor any agreement they entered. With concealed amusement, he chose to have a little fun in advance of possible negotiations.

"Well boys, that sounds good. It's about time you started thinking about moving out, getting you a fine woman and making a good life for yourself. I take it you have been saving your left-over crop income for the past few years. Now you can put that money to good use. Your daddy would be very proud."

Oris and Leonard glanced at each other as they tried hard not to show their disappointment. This was not exactly going the way they had anticipated. After a slight hesitation, they began to speak.

"We were really hoping you could help us out. We have saved some money. Still, we do not have the full amount needed to buy the property. It really is a good deal and we promise we will pay you back every cent."

Williford, who by this time was no longer able to maintain his stern facial expression, smiled and replied.

"Boys, I will be glad to help you make this purchase. Know that I expect you to work hard, spend your money wisely, and make your loan repayments on time. Are we in agreement?"

Amazed and delighted because of their uncle's willingness to help them, Oris and Leonard readily agreed.

"You will not be disappointed with us. We will honor your generosity and make you proud of us. Thank you so much!"

Once the property was purchased, the brothers decided to divide the land equally between them. There was a large farm house at one end of the property and a small country store at the opposite end. The brothers shared an equal desire to own and prosper from their investment. The specifics of what to do with their joint purchase were contritely different. Both were interested in farming the land; however, Leonard had absolutely no interest in operating a country store. Oris' desire to become a businessman prompted him to welcome the challenge of becoming a store proprietor. And thus, his journey began.

Chapter Two

"RED BIRD"

The original "Red Bird"

A small wood framed and unpainted building awaited the emergence of one excited young man with aspirations of opening his own business.

Lonnie Lloyd operated the small country store that was known as "The Red Bird." In addition to the services Lonnie provided for his customers, his brother, Richard Lloyd, operated a barber shop in the store. Richard cut hair for soldiers at Fort Bragg Army Base during the week. On Saturdays, he operated his barber shop in Lonnie's store and men would line up for haircuts.

Lonnie Lloyd

Even though the country was recovering from the Great Depression, Oris dared to accept the risky challenge of embarking on a career as proprietor of his own country store. He rented "Red Bird" for five dollars ($5.00) per month while he was having a new store constructed.

"Red Bird" was located adjacent to the baseball field where the Riley baseball team played against several other local community baseball teams. Crowds gathered every Saturday to cheer their teams on and frequented the "Red Bird" for their refreshments.

Chapter Three

NEW BUILDING CONSTRUCTED

The new store consisted of two floors, a side room, and a shelter across the front of the building. Oris changed the name "Red Bird" to "O.B. Gay's Store." The original "Red Bird" business was closed and the building used for storage and ice house. Richard moved his barbershop business into the new building and continued to cut hair until his death. Afterwards that part of the business was discontinued.

Oris continued to use the back room of the store for his residence. After thirteen months of camping out in the back of his store, Oris married Ruby Martin. They moved into the farm house that was on the property until their new home was constructed about two hundred feet behind his store. Construction of these two buildings resulted in some changes being made to the existing ballfield. The Gay's home now rested on the space previously designated as "third base" and the store rested on the "home base" area.

A few adjustments were made to base locations on the ball field and "The County Line Ball Club" still played baseball on Wednesdays and Saturdays. Mr. Lonnie Lloyd continued to purchase the baseballs used for the games and he remained as overseer of the games being played.

Fifty plus years later, when we were emptying the contents of the store and readying the building for upheaval, we discovered one of the

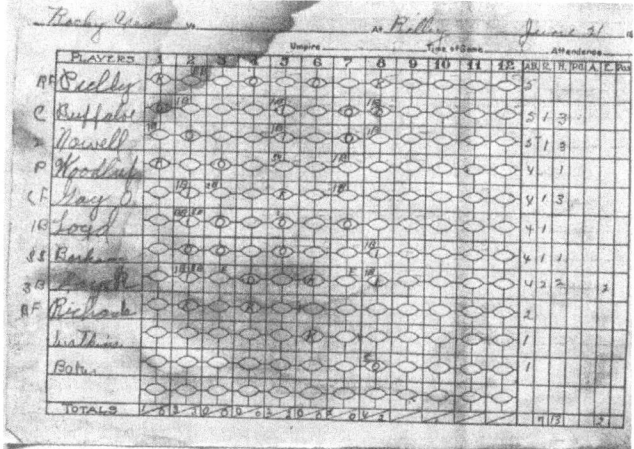

original score books used at those baseball games. The year of the book was 1936, the players' names and their scores were written in pencil and, to our pleasant surprise, the information remained very legible. The copy shown above reveals those players and their scores for the June 21,

1936 game played between Riley (County Line Ball Club) and Rocky Cross. Riley, the home team, had an impressive win. The home players were: Bill Pulley, Buffaloe, Ben Nowell, Woodlief, Oris Gay, Lloyd, Barham, Russell Gay, Richards, Watkins and Baker. Rocky Cross, the opposing team players, were: P. Massey, R. Murray, H. Murray, C. Pace, B. Strickland, Pearce, Brantley, M.L. Hagwood and Fields.

A binding friendship and mutual respect between Lonnie and Oris remained constant for years to come, until the death of Lonnie. Oris strived to continue the friendly and honest customer relationships for which his predecessor was so well known and respected. This was his way of honoring a man he so admired.

Once the land had been formally divided and the proportions agreed upon, Leonard and his wife, Ruth, moved into the house vacated by Oris and Ruby. A newly-constructed home, in conjunction with store building construction costs, constituted increased debt for Oris. Ultimately, this resulted in years of struggling to satisfy his credit obligations. Nonetheless, this dilemma never deterred his determination to endure and withstand the trials that evolved during those Depression Years in America.

Oris and Ruby

Side by side for the next fifty years, Oris and Ruby enjoyed working together in their store. Daddy's favorite pastime was bird hunting and fishing. Mother had no problem stepping in and running the store so that he could escape the pressures of the day. He enjoyed relaxing in his boat on his family's ten-acre pond or walking through the fields with a shotgun on his shoulder and his trusty bird dogs ahead of him searching for the prey.

He employed only three individuals, other than Mother of course, when the need arose. Wilton Gay left his home when he was just a teenager and worked in the store with Daddy. He also resided in the back room until he enlisted in service and went off to war. In addition to Wilton, two other individuals manned the store when Daddy was on a trip to haul tobacco, buy a truck load of oil burners, or drive Mother and me to Raleigh for our Saturday shopping. These men were Floyd Gay, daddy's uncle, and Roy Mitchell, daddy's first cousin. With the help of these individuals, his store operation was off to a smooth start.

Floyd Gay

Roy Mitchell

Chapter Four

"BUBBLE" GAS PUMP FILLING STATION

    Daddy's country store was referred to by some as a "service station" and others as a "filling station," implying gasoline could be purchased there. He simply called his business O. B. Gay's Store. It was, in fact, both a service and a filling station for he serviced the community and filled the needs of his customers.

    The store was a long, rectangular building with a side room attachment, both covered by tin siding. In the front of the store was a portico supported by two large cedar posts, grounded in a cement pillar, with a cement slab stretching from one pillar to the other.

    On this slab, there was a green Sinclair "bubble" gas pump. When the customer asked for the number of gallons of gas they needed, the attendant pulled back and forth on the manual pump to pump the gas from the underground tank into the "bubble" on top of the gas pump. Once the desired amount was visible in the clear glass cylinder, usually two to five gallons, the attendant placed the hose into the customer's vehicle and allowed the gas to flow into their gas tank.

    Also, on this slab, was a large, square green metal container which housed kerosene. On top of the tank was a hand pump for dispensing the desired amount of kerosene. Self-service was optional for use of this equipment; however, most of the customers preferred for the store attendant to provide the service.

    Eventually the bubble top gas pump was replaced by two gas pumps which computed the cost and displayed the amount on the face of the pumps. Customers could purchase either "regular" gas or "high test" gas. Most of the time they drove up on the outside lane of the tanks; however, when there was inclement weather, they chose to drive under the sheltered side lane.

    On the front outside wall of the side room, there was an air compressor with a hose attached. This pump was used more for inflating bicycle tires than vehicle tires, with one exception. Every Saturday afternoon, Jean, Betty Lou and Joyce Privette made sure their car tires were ready for a fun-filled ride.

    Adjacent to the side-room, there was an embankment along the road. In conjunction with the service station aspect of the store, Daddy had a space shoveled out of the embankment wide enough to drive the front or rear end of a car over it. He cemented each side of the top of the embankment. Customers could drive onto the cement and place their vehicle over the shoveled-out section. There they changed the oil and greased their car or truck.

Over the years, the demand for kerosene dwindled and the pump was removed. The air pump barely had enough pressure to inflate a tire and the air hose dry-rotted; thus, that service was discontinued.

The dirt roads were paved in the early 1950's; and, in the process, the embankment necessitated a reduction in height. Thus, the grease pit no longer availed.

Fewer customers stopped for gasoline because they could purchase it cheaper near their workplace in the cities or towns. The filling station part of the store diminished.

Chapter Five

POST-DEPRESSION YEARS' SALES

While cleaning out sections of the store's attic in the late 1960s, we discovered a cigar box in which were housed hand-written, in pencil, the amount of sales income for each day. These figures were written on a piece of cardboard and represented a sales-receipt accounting for the first two months of operation in O.B. Gay's store.

Though we found the figures barely legible, we still managed to successfully interpret them. To preserve the information, I took the sales slips to work with me the following day. Utilizing the availability of office equipment at my disposal, I placed them face down on the large, upright copier to enhance the readability of the recorded information. Once the copy processed and the finished product dropped into the tray located on the side of the machine, I pulled-back the rubberized covering to retrieve the originals. The heat from the lamp crossing the scanned area, combined with the age of the papers, caused the sales slips to disintegrate when I attempted to remove them. Thankfully, legible copies were made of each slip before the information was destroyed.

December 1933 sales totaled $838.51. During the month of January 1934, sales ranged from $8.50 per day to $54.00 per day. The total January sales came to $629.85. My daddy was off to a good start with a total of $1,468.36 for his first two months of operation in his store.

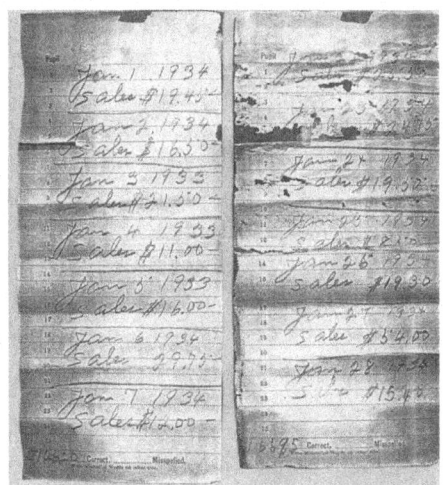

These sales were not derived totally from large sale items; rather, they also included countless numbers of items purchased for a penny, a nickel, a dime, or a quarter. Nabs and peanuts, moon pies, etc. sold for five cents a pack. Soda pops were five cents each and you could buy six for a quarter. At those rates, the old cash register rang continuously throughout each day to arrive at the sales totals presented above.

These sales were good considering people and businesses were optimistic of a future filled with more prosperity. *Back in the Day* booklets from Hallmark for the year 1933 revealed that "The 1933 overall average income was $1,136.00 per year. Teachers averaged $1,300.00 per year, coal miners $900.00, clerical $889.00, manufacturing $1,170.00, construction $942.00, and retail employee $1,083.00. A new house cost $5,755.00 and a new car cost $652.00."

Larger stores, too, were recovering from years of depression and resorted to bargain sales prices to move their merchandise. According to *Back in the Day 1933,* "An International Harvester 2-ton truck was a bargain at $995.00." Newspaper advertisements during this period featured a list of "practical gifts" which could be purchased at Charles Stores Company in Raleigh, N. C.

According to the sales advertisements in a December 31, 1933 News and Observer, "Ladies bedroom slippers sold for 39 cents, crepe slippers were 50 cents and new high-heel fall shoes were $1.98 per pair. Women's handbags were 29 cents and their silk hose was 79 cents per pair. Alarm clocks were 89 cents, infant's sweaters were 69 cents, and fruit cakes were 29 cents. Women's 'bloomers' sold for 35 cents, women's gloves were 39 cents and men's gloves were $1.00. The final gift special offered was a sport wrist watch for $2.69."

Another store advertised a great annual sale of furniture. "Baby cribs were $7.90, linoleum rugs were $2.29, mattresses were $3.98, a studio couch was $26.95, kitchen table and chair set was $14.45. A complete living room suite was $49.75, a complete bedroom suite was $39.85, and a complete dining room suite was $119.00." Additionally, "bed springs and mattress outfits were $10.98, end tables were 97 cents; lastly, towels were 19 cents and 29 cents each."

A&P grocery stores featured such products as "butter for 27 cents, 2 pint bottles of grape juice for 25 cents, sliced bread (16 oz. loaf) for 6 cents, package of flakes for 15 cents, peas were 2 cans for 35 cents, and Eight O'clock coffee sold for 15 cents per pound. Ivory soap sold for 11 cents for two medium cakes. Plain or self-rising flour was 85 cents for a 24-pound bag. Sugar was 49 cents for a 10-pound bag. Pork hams sold for 15 cents per pound and pork shoulders for 11 cents per pound. Smithfield hams sold for 31 cents per pound. Oysters were 35 cents per quart and lettuce was 8 and ½ cents for one large hard head. Celery was 8 and ½ cents for a large crisp stalk. Cranberries sold for 12 and ½ cents per quart and fancy red emperor grapes were 7 and ½ cents per pound."

"Back In The Day" booklets I purchased at Hallmark provided a condensed review of prices for different years. I chose the 1933 booklet and the 1983 booklet to provide a comparative.

	1933	1983
Gasoline per gallon	18 cents	$1.24
Eggs per dozen	29 cents	89 cents
Butter per pound	28 cents	$2.06
Bread per loaf	07 cents	54 cents
Coffee per pound	26 cents	$2.47
Potatoes per 10 lbs.	23 cents	$2.06
Milk per gallon	41 cents	$2.26
Bacon per pound	23 cents	$1.94
Sugar per 5 pounds	27 cents	$1.81

Chapter Six

POST-DEPRESSION YEARS' PROMOS

While the country was still recovering from the depression years, advertisers scurried to create ideas that would lure the consuming public into purchasing their products. What then materialized was the presumptive idea that with some products the consumer could receive "something for nothing." With these marketing gimmicks, advertisers catered not only to adults but children as well. In some cases, gift catalogs were provided displaying a wide array of gift items for free with the exchange of coupons, wrappers, or trademark symbols, to name a few.

Cigarette companies encouraged people to smoke pack after pack and collect coupons that were attached to each one. This was years before cigarettes packs carried required health issue warnings; and, at this period in history, they were not frowned upon by the public. Two of the popular brands purchased from Daddy's store were Raleigh regular brand cigarettes and Bel Air menthol brand. Those who bought cigarettes by the carton, as opposed to by the single pack, received extra bonus coupons with their purchase. Customers collected these coupons and when they reached the required number needed to exchange for an item in the gift catalog they redeemed them. One couple, who weekly purchased these cigarettes, saved and exchanged them for garden and lawn equipment, from water hoses to practical tools, for their yard. They explained,

"The products we received were always of good quality and they lasted for many years. We were always pleased with our exchange gifts."

Boxes of laundry and dish detergent contained glasses, dishes, or kitchen towels. Duz detergent provided either a cup, a saucer, or a plate in each box. The more boxes you purchased the better your chances of finally completing a full set of dishes with the gold-colored wheat pattern beautifully displayed; and, after all it came "free," right?

In the 1940's, collectible bird cards could be found in the Arm & Hammer Baking Soda boxes. Each card had a colorful picture of a bird and information about the bird's size, breeding habits and territory. The White-breasted Nuthatch card was a "prize" given to me in 1948 at my pre-school registration at Wakelon Elementary School in Zebulon, N.C.

Write Right composition books and note book filler paper appealed to both adults and children. Each book or pack of filler paper had a Write Right trade mark coupon on it and could be exchanged for prizes. For ten Write Right coupons and twenty cents you could get a miniature flashlight or a ball point pen, or an identification bracelet. For ten Write Right coupons and fifteen cents you could get a compass ring or a magic mirror mask. Teachers were encouraged to save these coupons and win big cash prizes from $10 to the grand prize of $200.

Covers from Blue Horse composition books and Lucky

Star composition books had a trademark coupon on the cover which could also be exchanged for gifts. Prizes were a little different from the Write Right ones but the exchange amounts were basically the same.

Ice cream companies offered a variety of prize exchange opportunities. Small cups of ice cream cost only five cents and had a treasure under the lid. Once you licked the ice cream off the lid and very carefully removed the plastic covering, there before your eager eyes was revealed the exciting moment when you discovered which famous movie star's face appeared on the lid. Carefully laying the lid aside, it was time to grasp the small wooden spoon and delve into that delicious cup of ice cream.

The ice cream delivery truck had folders with twenty-four wide slots in them. Each time you collected a movie star cup lid, you placed it in a slot. When you filled the entire card with twenty-four pictures, you could then exchange it for an 8X10 glossy picture of a favorite movie star of your choice.

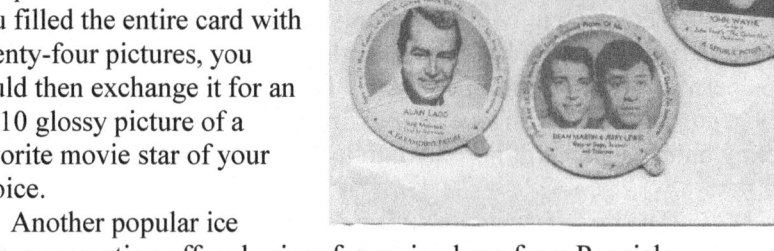

Another popular ice cream promotion offered prizes for saving bags from Popsicle, Fudgsicle, Creamsicle and Dreamsicle. Children were encouraged to save the ice cream on-a-stick bags with polka dots and

"Popsicle Pete" and exchange these bags for gifts. A comic-book-like catalog was provided from which to choose their gifts. 200 bags or 50 cents and 25 bags could be exchanged for a baseball; 100 bags or 20 cents and 10 bags for an initial ring or a bike horn; 475 bags or $1.00 and 25 bags for a camera; 600 bags or $1.35 and 25 bags for a baby doll; 70 bags or 15 cents and 10 bags for a telescope or midget harmonica, and for 70 bags or 15 cents and 10 bags you could get an exotic string of simulated pearls, seventeen inches long with a fashionable clasp. That was just a few of the prizes offered for collecting these bags.

Cracker Jack, the caramel-coated mixture of popcorn and peanuts, offered a prize nesting somewhere in each box sold. Most of the time it was located at the very bottom of the box. Kids soon became wise to that practice and either opened the box from the bottom or poured the contents out to see their prize before they ate the Cracker Jacks. Generations kept these little plastic figures and added them to their colorful collections. Duplicates were often exchanged with friends to expand the variety in their collections.

Bubble-gum cards were another popular purchase for collecting. In the 1930's there were movie star pictures on the cards. By the 1950's cards appealed to the adolescents when they offered cards with comic book heroes, television and sports stars. Early television "spanned" bubble gum cards featuring western legends. By the 1960's Elvis Presley bubble gum cards appeared, followed by several other rock and roll stars.

1933, "The Lone Ranger debuts on American radio" and immediately paraphernalia bearing that name flooded the retail market.

By the 1940's there was a Lone Ranger chewing gum that was popular. Each package contained a colored card that showed The Lone Ranger in action. However, the most widely known Lone Ranger advertisements were from the Merita Bread Baking Company.

As part of its advertising campaign during the 1940's and 1950's, Merita Bread provided screen doors for both the front and back of the store on which they displayed their name.

The company also provided calendars displaying The Lone Ranger and Merita Bread on it. The Lone Ranger was sitting on his white horse, Silver, just above a loaf of Merita Bread which was captioned, "It's Enriched by Merita Bread."

Metal signs with the same picture and caption were distributed to store owners to be used as advertising mechanisms and displayed on the wall of their store. The wall signs, unlike the calendars, did not include a caption above The Lone Ranger stating, "Watch the Lone Ranger Saturday Mornings on CBS."

Merita offered some Lone Ranger gifts such as a board where you made your way around the "trail" in a competition using cut-out small loaves of bread to place on whatever space you landed after your latest spin. This board was much like the other board games of the time such as Uncle Wiggly or Monopoly.

During this period, Lone Ranger comic books were readily available. Unless you were a member of The Lone Ranger Safety Club, the coveted Merita Bread Lone Ranger Pencil Sharpener was not available. My utmost desire was to own one of those pencil sharpeners. Unfortunately for me, my parents were against sending money to join a club.

We had one of the nicest Merita Bread delivery men. He always took time to talk with me and the other kids in the store while we fired questions about, whom else but, The Lone Ranger. One Saturday morning I asked him,

"Is there any way I can get one of those silver bullet pencil sharpeners without joining a club?"

He replied,

"Well, let me check into that and see what I can find out."

Satisfied with his answer, I left him to his delivery chores and went out the back door of the store and headed to the house.

Later that evening when Daddy came to the house for supper, he removed a bright and shiny Lone Ranger silver bullet pencil sharpener from his pocket and placed it on the table.

I looked at him with shocked disbelief and questioned,

"Where did you get that pencil sharpener? May I please have it?"

He smiled and handed it to me.

"After the bread man finished stacking the shelves with fresh bread, he went out to his truck again. When he returned, he handed the pencil sharpener to me and asked me to give it to you."

I was ecstatic over the gift. Now I was more convinced than ever that our Merita Bread delivery man was The Lone Ranger without his mask and horse. How else could he so easily come up with a silver bullet?

Many years passed and our bread man retired from the route. He and his wife visited the store shortly after his retirement. He introduced her to us, turned to me, and then said to his wife,

"This is the young lady I told you about; the one who always believed I was The Lone Ranger in disguise."

We all had a big laugh and a pleasant visit with my "hero" and his wife. Just like it is with "Santa Clause," part of me still wanted to believe he really was "The Lone Ranger."

Chapter Seven

HE CUT THE CHEESE

This expression has taken on a derogatory meaning over the years; but, for this writing, it refers to slicing a piece of cheese from the "hoop" and presenting it to the customer for consumption.

Produce and staples did not come prepackaged during the beginning years of O. B. Gay's store operation. Customers stepped up to the counter and expressed their desire for a specific measurement or certain weight of the product they wished to purchase. One of the food items in highest demand was the hoop cheese. Daddy bought two or three boxes of cheese each time the Henderson, NC salesman took his order. He always bought Wisconsin cheese and that milder cheddar seemed to be the cheese of choice for his customers. In addition, they were very adamant that their choice cut of hoop cheese be the exact weight they wanted.

Thank goodness Daddy was proficient in math because accurate measurement was a prerequisite for satisfying the customer. And when it came time to cut the cheese, a steady hand was a welcomed asset.

Daddy took the hoop cheese down from the shelf, removed the wooden cover and reached for his long knife. With both the precision and accuracy of a skilled surgeon, he placed the knife on the top of the cheese and firmly pushed the blade through it. He paused, stepped back from the cheese and determined the exact angle he needed to make his next cut to complete the process. Those around him watched in awe when he removed the cut slice from the block of cheese and placed it on the scales. He smiled when the reading on the scales revealed an exact, to-the-ounce, perfect cut. Some of the men bought a second or third slice of cheese just to challenge him. They wondered,

"Could he cut that cheese in the exact portioned weight and not go over or under the desired amount?"

As usual, he met their challenge. He even pocketed extra sales income in the process.

Customers expected that same exactness in their other purchases such as flour or sugar. These staples were usually delivered to the store in twenty-five and fifty pound sacks. Some customers purchased the full sacks; others preferred to purchase only their desired amount, which would be scooped from the larger sacks and poured into a smaller paper bag. These bags usually held from two to five pounds of flour or sugar. Once the bags were filled, they were weighed for the customer's approval. Finally, a string was securely tied around the top of the filled bag to prevent spillage.

For customers with a sweet tooth, coconuts were another commodity in demand. To meet the request for a bag of shredded coconut, more exact measurements were incorporated.

The coconuts were delivered to the store in large, air-vented bags. Daddy picked a coconut from the bag and examined it carefully to check for firmness or spoilage. He turned it until he located the end that had the dark indentions. Usually there were two or three indentions that presented a face-like appearance; plus, they indicated the weakest places on the coconut. They would be utilized to extract the juice of the coconut before the process of pounding and grinding began.

Daddy used a hammer and an ice pick to penetrate the coconut's shell and drain the juice out of it. Once he successfully pried a hole in the shell, he turned the coconut upside down over a fruit jar and allowed the juice to drain. He punched a hole in both ends of the coconut so there would be an even flow. After it was drained of all juice, he placed it on a wood cutting board and began bashing it with a hammer in an effort to crack it open.

Once the coconut cracked open, he took a knife and pried the meat away from inside the shell. He made sure to scrape that last thin layer of clinging shell that wanted to be stubborn and refuse to release the meat. He removed the small wire basket that was hanging by a tobacco-twine rope from the ceiling and filled it with the coconut meat pieces. He placed the pieces into the hand crank grinder. Rhythmically, he turned the crank of the grinder and shred the pieces. He scooped the finished product from the container beneath the grinder and placed it in the bucket-scale. The customer requested amount measured accurately. He bagged it and presented it to his customer. Coconut shredded this way remained fresh and was ideal for baking cakes and pies. The drained juice which had been placed into a container was then presented to the customer to pour over the coconut before baking.

An equally popular purchase was bananas. Exact weight purchases of this fruit can be made in grocery stores today by placing a small batch of five to seven bananas on a scale and determining the desired amount. However, the bananas sold in Daddy's store were grown in clusters and hung from the top of a stalk. They were green when delivered to the store and usually were in two separate large bundles wrapped in a plastic covering. Customers pulled the bananas from the stalk, often before they were ripe, and purchased them individually. Some customers with large families to feed bought a full stalk instead of single banana purchases. Then they carried the stalk home and hung it up in their kitchen pantry where family members enjoyed at their leisure.

Along the same line of merchandise being delivered to the store, one customer, C.A. Lloyd, remembered crackers in a barrel: "Crackers came in a fifty-pound blue barrel that was twenty-four inches in diameter and about waist-high. Me and Pete Privette ate crackers every day."

A different weight measure was employed for molasses this time in liquid rather than solid form. Pint, quart, half-gallon or gallon jars were the methods of choice used by customers to purchase molasses. The molasses was delivered to the store in fifty gallon wooden barrels. They were placed on a platform and turned on their side. A hand pump was placed on the barrel to pump the molasses into the jar. Again, the intent was to fill the jar to the exact jar level the customer requested. Mother was not completely comfortable with that method; therefore, she placed a funnel in the jar top before pumping the molasses.

Last, but not least, there was the cast iron plug tobacco cutter. For those customers who loved the taste of tobacco but preferred not to smoke cigarettes, there was the option of a plug of chewing tobacco. They broke off a small piece of the plug and placed it in the jaw of their mouth. Then they chewed on it until the mixture of saliva and chewed-up tobacco caused them to draw a dead aim and hurl a "wad" into the spittoon.

Wholesale distributers sold this chewing tobacco in "brick" form to the stores. The customers, in turn, purchased "plugs" from this brick. A cutter was used to measure and cut off the desired plug size.

To accomplish this feat, Daddy used a cast iron plug tobacco cutter. He placed the tobacco brick securely on the lower frame part of the cutter just below where the scooped-out, angled blade would strike. The actual cutter apparatus and the way he administered the cutting procedure was reminiscent of the blade thrusting of a miniature guillotine.

Daddy pulled back on the blade handle and, with a swift and powerful vertical motion, he applied the sharp blade to the brick. In the process, he managed to cutoff the precisely measured plug of chewing tobacco for his customer.

These are just a few of the personal, hands-on sales practices of yesteryear that contrast the prepackaged, impersonal sales practices of today. The "artistry" has been replaced by the "robot."

Chapter Eight

DIVERSIFICATION, DETERMINATION, DEDICATION

My daddy, Oris, believed in diversification and was unwilling to lead a mundane existence. He was a man who wore many hats. Not only was he a farmer and a merchant, but he was also the local fertilizer distributor and transporter and installer of Florence Mayo oil burners for the local farmers' barns.

School was out for the summer and I looked forward to climbing up into his 1949 two-ton stake bed Ford truck. I would lean far out the side window and attempt to adjust the huge rear-view exterior mirror. Feat accomplished, I became excited because he was going to allow me to accompany him on his ride to Farmville, NC to pick up a load of oil burners. I enjoyed walking through the warehouse and marveling at the many rows of newly manufactured pieces of equipment being prepared for farmers to use in curing tobacco. My favorite memory of these trips was when Daddy would stop at The Rock Side in Middlesex and buy some of the most delicious hotdogs in the world. Little did I know at the time just how close by this restaurant was. This was the highlight of a long trip with daddy to secure a truckload of oil burners.

In the fall of each year, Daddy wore another hat. Tobacco auctioneers and warehouse owners from Oxford, NC, Wilson NC, Greenville, NC and Clarksville, Va. frequently visited his store. These men encouraged Daddy to choose their warehouse for the designated market to which he hauled the local farmers' tobacco for sale. Daddy became the trustee of thousands of dollars from the sale of tobacco crops until he could safely deliver the money to the awaiting farmers upon his return from the market. These farmers trusted his judgement in assuring their product received a fair and just price. They were confident of his honesty, integrity, and with the management decisions he made on their behalf. Additionally, they welcomed his prudent delivery of funds from their sales.

No matter what professional hat Daddy wore at any given time, the one thing that remained evident was the trust and confidence his constituents placed in him. His policy of honesty was the key to his success in each of his endeavored fields of work.

Even though he gained respect for his diversification and dedication in serving the community, there were those who took advantage of his mild manner. They failed to uphold their end of the bargain when it came to paying him for his services or for goods they charged at his store. He would ask for his money only once. If the creditors ignored or refused his request, he moved on and never took any legal actions to collect from them. I remember one individual who charged groceries and necessities for his family of six children for the entire year. When his crop was sold and time came for him to honor his obligation and satisfy the outstanding debt, he walked into the store and adamantly blurted:

"Yeah, I sold my tobacco but there is no money to pay store bills. I have a family to feed the rest of this year and into crop time next year. You will just have to wait. My family is not going to go without eating even if you never get your money!"

He stormed back out the front door and, once again, Daddy never received compensation for his generosity and trust.

When another customer, Dan, was confronted about a fertilizer bill he argued,

"I didn't buy that much fertilizer from you and I'm not paying you another cent!"

Daddy, unlike other country store proprietors in the area, did not require the customer to sign or initial the sales ticket at the time of the original charge. Unfortunately, "The Golden Rule" was not practiced by some of his patrons.

Daddy responded,

"Well I guess you are calling me and Ruby crooked liars. Some of the tickets were written by her and the others by me, depending on who was working when you got the fertilizer. Go on, get out of here! If you can live with stealing, I can live with being stolen from."

That was the only time I remember hearing my daddy stand up to a "deadbeat."

Then there was Nick who, when being presented with his outstanding bill, stated,

"That lawnmower I bought from you back in the spring is worn out and I can't use it anymore. It won't run so I don't see why you think I should pay you for it!"

Once again, Daddy's refusal to require ticket signing cost him money. He felt a man's word was sufficient. Therefore, when he was confronted by a customer who was unwilling to pay, he just took his loss and continued…even allowing some of those returning "deadbeats" to charge again the next year. Other merchants in the area often criticized him for not being stern and for being a "pushover." Though these merchants ran a tighter charge/pay policy, and thereby were more successful in realizing a large profit, Daddy's practices endured the test of time. Years after other establishments closed their doors and went out of business, the man referred to as "weak" in his business practices became "the last man standing" as he celebrated his fifty-year anniversary in his capacity as proprietor of his country store.

Chapter Nine

OLD SALES SLIPS WEAVE PICTORIAL HISTORY

Credit cards and debit cards were unheard of during the formative years of this country store business. To keep the store operational during the post-depression era, farmers were afforded credit through the months leading up to the end of tobacco harvesting season. Once the farmers sold their crops, those who were reputable enough to honor their promise to pay would satisfy their "word agreement" debt obligation as promised. However, a large safe lined with rows of paper charge slips could be found. Some of those tickets contained a single charge of five cents for a soda. These small amounts were the most unpaid charges when customers returned on their next visit to the store. Decades later, when the store finally closed, stacks of those single-item charge slips remained in the old upright, metal hangers found in the steel safe.

Stained and dusty sales slips found in the old store safe presented a pictorial history of five decades of changes. As I shook the dust and flipped through those old sales slips, it became evident these items represented a time when life was not so complicated and people were less hurried. Visions of an informal lifestyle emerged. Items in demand consisted of life necessities with little or no emphasis placed on luxuries. Some people paid for needed purchases with cash money. Those who had no cash paid for merchandise with credit. Other times, the barter system was implemented for goods. Some of the ladies in the neighborhood would gather eggs, place them in wooden crates and send their children to the store to exchanges for goods. Most often these items for exchange included such staples as flour, sugar, other food items or household supplies. If the child was lucky, sometimes there might have been enough left for a piece of penny candy. Even if there wasn't, Daddy was known to have slipped a small paper bag to the child, told him or her to get some candy and be sure to "eat it before you get back home."

Upon further examination of those old sales slips, I was able to determine what time of year the purchases were made. During the summer months, people bought drinks, moon pies, ice cream, and sherbets. The men bought tobacco products and farm products such as harnesses for the mules and farm tools. People purchased more gas for their vehicles so they could take their "Sunday afternoon drive."

During the winter months, sales centered on the animals. There were salt blocks for the mules, large bags of feed for the chickens, cows, and pigs. You could always tell when it was hog killing time because there was a demand for lard stands and large buckets. Other purchases consistent with winter time were hammers, nails, axes, ax handles, galvanized buckets, kerosene, wicks and matches for the lanterns.

Then came springtime and with it seed purchases of all kinds. Planting time included vegetable seeds, flower seeds, tobacco, and cotton seeds. Rakes, hoes, pitch forks, and replacement handles were in demand. In addition, the ladies bought brooms, mops, dusters, and various cleaning products used in their spring cleaning. For those fortunate enough to relax by the pond, purchases of long-cane-fishing poles and roles of string, along with different lures (for those who did not dig up fishing worms in their back yard) necessary for the "catch of the day."

During the spring months, some customers came into the store dressed in shirts or dresses made from the feed bag prints they had purchased the previous winter. Sales slips projected countless rolls of thread, cards of needles and boxes of buttons used to turn those feed bags into beautiful wearing apparel. Without question, these season-represented sales slips presented a picture of a time when life was ordinary and people were self-dependent and easy to please.

Chapter Ten

GATHER AROUND THE STOVE

A.O. Gay & Russell Gay

Throughout fifty years' operation of this store, one thing remained constant, the laughter and the lies shared among the customers circling around the old potbellied stove. During the cold months of winter, whether Daddy filled the stove with wood or coal, diligence was required to assure the fire was warm and toasty when the customers arrived. When the smoke weaved its way up the long pipe that ran through the high-beamed ceiling and penetrated the attic area, a message of "welcome" escaped the roof and filled the air. Even the long wooden floors, with their weathered and worn gaps, fell prey to the coldness from outside.

Friends and neighbors were greeted as they gathered:

"Do drop in," grab yourself a drink and a moon pie," "pull up a nail keg and set for a spell," and swap a few "loafers' lodge" yarns around the old stove. These were a few of the greetings encountered when a customer entered the store.

Some of the men had a taste for "Chew-tobacco," and others had a taste for "snuff." To accommodate these individuals when they encountered the need to dispose of a "wad," a wooden box was provided as a spittoon. This box was an empty hoop-cheese box, filled with sand from outside, where upon those who were inclined to empty their tobacco or snuff-filled jaw could do so in the manner of a baseball pitcher's "spit" before a pitch. To me, this was absolutely disgusting, ugh!

When the men came in around lunch time and ordered a can of sardines and some crackers, I had to place the can flat down on the shelf, pull the elongated handle of the can opener over the can, and puncture a hole in the top. With each turn of the hand-operated handle, the fishy smell of those raw sardines floated in the air. With my breath held, I managed to open the can and hand it to the customer. Often, I made a fast exit out the back door for a breath of fresh air before opening a can for the next customer in line. Double Ugh!

The topic of the day was often not unlike the topics of today, from the sweltering heat to the blistering cold. Unlike today, there was no air conditioning to run to in the summer; rather, there was a shade tree or an open window with a large fan in it to provide cooling. In the winter, there was no central heating system. Instead, there was the wood or coal-burning potbellied stove. The men with their laid-back bodies and out-stretched legs soaked up the warmth from the hot stove. Instead of "what I saw on television last night," the conversations usually were about "what the old lady heard at the quilting bee last night."

Political discussions, unlike today, were seldom the topic of debate. Conversations included crop planting and harvesting and the weather conditions determining the successful production of their crops. Hunting, fishing, trapping, baseball and the latest hot gossip rounded out an evening of verbal exchanges.

Daddy was an advocate of both hunting and fishing. Whether he had his 12-gauge shotgun and his trusty dog or had his fishing pole and his Chevy truck, he could compete with the best of them.

Hunting was a popular topic

discussed around the circle. Listening to those men talk, one would think they would be willing to trade their own wife for a trusty bird dog. Opening day of dove and quail hunting season was more exciting to them than Christmas morning for the kids. Waking up at dawn, enduring whatever weather condition prevailed, they would walk for hours through muddy fields and brush woods in search of birds, rabbits, foxes, etc. The bird hunters took extra precaution not to move too close and spook the prey before their dog either "pointed" or "set" and waited for their owner to move in for the kill. At the end of the day, the hunters would head back to the country store. Here they would swap stories about how many prey they killed and how many they managed to get "with just one shot."

The fishing stories being told carried a little less reliability than those hunting stories. Someone once said,

"They had a fishing worm at the end of the line and a crazy fool at the end of the pole."

Fool or not, to these men fishing was the ultimate means of relaxation. Spinning their fish yarns was the highlight of their evening when gathered with friends at the old country store.

Durwood Mitchell

Leonard Gay

For those customers who had little interest in talk swap, a couple of nail kegs and a handmade table made for checkers provided their entertainment. In another corner of the store, you could find a small table set up for the evening's round of cards. (Found among remnants at the closing of the store was a pack of cards that had been played so much you could barely recognize what face or number appeared on the card.)

Another form of relaxation utilized while visiting the side room of the store was the trusty old "pool" (billiards) table. Sometimes during the day, when there were only one or two customers playing pool, one of  the men would attempt to teach me how to play. He placed a small step-stool beside the pool table. I was not tall enough to see over the pool table and that was the only way I could play. They said I played a "mean" game of pool. Somehow, I find that highly doubtful. However, my vocabulary increased as I learned new words and expressions from the pool lessons I was taught. Sometimes, I was instructed to "put a little 'English' spin on the ball." Other times, a suggestion was made that I "run the table by sinking all fifteen balls."

Amid the yarn swapping, the humorous tales, the occasional splatter of tobacco as it landed in the sand-filled cheese box beneath the stove, sometimes heated conversations erupted.

Daddy seldom had time to participate in the conversations. He listened and let them talk. He was a good-natured, happy individual who seldom exhibited any anger. However, the one thing that would get him riled was profanity and foul language being uttered in the presence of a lady, especially his wife or daughter. The mild-mannered little merchant turned into a red-faced angry tyrant. I once witnessed him as he grabbed one man by the shirt collar, turned him around, pushed him to the front door, raised his foot up and literally kicked the man out the door.

"Don't come back through that door until you learn how to talk around the women!"

Then he turned and walked back to the cash register like nothing happened. There was quietness in the store for a while. When the conversations did continue, there were no more unruly words spoken.

Chapter Eleven

HIDDEN AWAY QUIET AS A MOUSE

In the early fifties, a wall was erected in the rear of the store, housing an area of privacy to enable the proprietor to manage his daily purchase and sales receipts.

On the back wall of this area was a huge, heavy metal-like safe consisting of six pull-out trays with rows of sturdy clamps under which customer charge tickets were placed. An eight-foot-long wooden desk with a slanted top and one elongated drawer provided the needed work space. At the far end of this desk was a large, fire-proof safe on rollers. The interior walls of the safe were so thick there was only room enough to utilize a small shoebox storage space. The safe was very heavy and required three muscular men to move it into the store. The flooring beneath was nothing short of utmost sturdiness or the safe would surely have fallen through as a result of the extreme weight. A structured sheet of wire was attached to the rear of the desk top and extended about five feet high. Approximately two feet in front of the desk, the wall separating the office from the customer area had a row of four sliding clear-glass windows. These windows provided store-activity monitoring for the proprietor.

Consumed with curiosity over the conversations held among the men gathered in the store, I often entered the back door, ducked down so I would not be noticed, and quietly crawled under the desk to listen to talk coming from the other side of the separation wall. I remained "hidden away" and focused my undivided attention on what those men were discussing. They sat around the stove or stood along the back on the wall beyond where I was hiding and were never without an interesting tale to talk about.

The little corner where they gathered to talk could today probably be referred to as their "man cave." The women did not accompany their husbands to the store. Instead, the women and children would join Mother and me at the house until the men were ready to return home. Other times, the husbands would drop their wife off at a quilting bee on their way to the store. Once they left the store, they would pick her up from the "bee" and head home. The men never told the women about the store gossip; but, they eagerly listened to find out what the women talked that night. Then, they could hardly wait until the next night when, back at the store, they could spread the latest gossip that "the ole lady heard at the quilting bee last night."

Not all their topics included fishing and hunting or the success and problems of their field crops. Other topics included baseball games or sometimes the local high school athletics. Seldom did one of the sessions end without a discussion about the indiscretions of some people in the community. Occasionally, some verbal exchanges could be perceived as scandalous. While I listened intensely to the "gossip" being exchanged, I sometimes had to cover my mouth; but, it wasn't because what I heard shocked me. Rather, I was frantically trying to keep from sneezing because of the cluttered boxes of dusty papers that surrounded me.

Sometimes I was joined by a scampering mouse that fled the front of the store and was seeking refuge underneath the wooden desk. Once he determined the human he encountered was no threat to him, he settled in his own corner of the floor area and we both remained "quiet as a mouse."

When the men gathered in the store, there was no differential between the labeled "church people" and those who had long since graced the entrance of a church. Some of the "juiciest" gossip often came from the lips of a deacon of the local churches. One "disclosure" stood out to me.

"Fellows, we had an interesting deacon meeting last week. You would not believe some of the things going on in this community. We had to dismiss one of our own for public display of drunkenness. Who would have ever thought he would do that?"

Another man joined in the conversation saying,

"Well, I know who you're talking about. His papa runs one of the biggest moonshine operations around."

"Maybe he was sampling papa's latest brew," he added with a chuckle.

Ignoring the interruption, the first man continued talking about the events of his deacons' meeting.

"Another man approached the board, declared he had learned the error of his ways, had repented, and wished to be reinstated. His membership was reinstated and he was welcomed back."

From across the room, someone blurted out,

"What did he do that was so bad in the first place?"

The deacon hesitated for a moment and then continued with his speech.

"Then we had a lady come forth who had been dismissed several months for being with child out of wedlock. She wished to be reinstated because her child had been born and she had changed her ways. She, too, was reinstated and welcomed back into the church."

After this, one of the men who had remained silent throughout these conversations, cleared his throat and, in a semi-excited tone, added his comments.

"Yeah, my old lady said she heard all about your meeting when she went to her quilting bee last night. She said you all dismissed two more women from the church because they were going to have a baby and they were not married either. Everybody stopped quilting. They were all shocked to hear about such 'shenanigans!' "

"Hmmph, didn't shock me none!" retorted another man in the group. He paused for a second and I could hear the thud as he spit a chew of tobacco into the spittoon beside the stove.

"I know which women your old lady was talking about. Heck, everybody knows there is always some hanky-panky going on whenever either one of them women is around. More than one man in this community could be the daddy of their child."

Noticing the irritated look on the men's faces, he added,

"Well, I'm just saying there is a lot more people don't know about."

Not to be out done, another man entered the discussion.

"I could probably tell y'all some things that would knock your socks off. This sort of thing is being talked about in all the stores around here. Believe me, there is a whole lot going on that has not been exposed yet."

Another replied,

"You don't say! So Mister Know-it-all, just who and what have you heard other people talking about?"

Maybe I was letting my imagination go at this point; but, there seemed to be a somewhat anxiousness coming from that last statement. A little bit of guilt, maybe? Interesting!

The last man continued,

"Better not open my big mouth too much. I don't want somebody to come up and accuse me of spreading gossip. It's best not to get involved."

A response of disgust came from a customer who had just joined the group; and, who obviously did not have a high opinion of the man who had just spoken.

"Just what I thought. You don't have a clue about anything going on behind closed doors. You are just blowing steam, as usual!"

"Oh yeah? I may not know everything going on behind closed doors but I sure as heck know what has been going on in the woods behind my tobacco field."

Another disbeliever retorted,

"Man this ought to be good! Why don't you tell us what is going on in the woods?"

With obvious anger in his voice, the challenged man spoke.

"Okay, Mr. Smarty Pants, get a load of this. When I was cleaning up some brush piles near the woods out back of my farm last week, I witnessed a shocking situation. One of our 'can do no wrong' neighbors drove down the path beside my tobacco field and pulled off into the woods. He turned his engine off, stepped out of his car, and opened the trunk. 'Lo and behold' out climbed that pretty widow woman that he has supposedly been helping with her finances since her husband passed away. The things they did next were a sight for sore eyes. I am glad they didn't spot me and come over to my brush pile. With all the heat in them woods, my brush pile would probably have turned into a big forest fire!"

Years later when a nighttime television soap opera, entitled "Peyton Place," aired, I would be reminded of those "juicy" subjects I overheard in Daddy's store.

These conversations and the direction in which they were headed forced one man who had remained silent throughout the discussions to speak out.

"These subjects need to be dropped. Frankly, I think this whole conversation is getting out of hand! We need to talk about something that's not so gossipy. Some of us just need to Shut Up!"

Enough said! That was the end of those conversations and the end of my listening to far-fetched accusations for one day. Whew!

In essence, there was humor attributed to these conversations and the countless others that followed over the years. Alas, just more proof that men often were bigger and better gossipers than women.

Other times, I was forced to suppress the urge to laugh at the one-liners and name calling exchanged. Various opinions of other people could easily have been described as sheer cruelty. One man obviously was not in agreement with his daughter's choice of a husband. He referred to his son-in-law,

"That scum is like a booger on your nose that you can't wipe off."

In a later conversation, one of the men referred to his next-door-neighbor,

"He struts about telling others what to do and acting like he is so great. Everybody knows he is the laziest man that ever walked. He is a good for nothing and ain't got the sense to see we are all laughing at him behind his back."

This vocal rendering was upsetting to me. I knew the person they were talking about and was shocked to hear how he was perceived by his neighbors and friends. Those country boys could be very cruel at times.

There were many uncomplimentary expressions used to describe others who frequented the store and exited only to be ridiculed by someone after they left. For instance, a very pleasant lady went out the front door of the store and immediately I heard giggling coming from two young boys standing near the back door.

"That old woman is uglier than homemade soap," one boy said as they continued to laugh.

The other boy added,

"She would be great at hog killing time. She's got enough fat to fill a tub of lard."

Both comments disgusted me but I wasn't surprised to hear comments such as that. After all, they were often exposed to negative comments from the adults talking about someone who had just exited the store.

"He's as sneaky as a yard snake."

"Yeah, he's sneaky alright. He thinks he is slick. Just like a greasy old eel."

Other descriptive terms often overheard were "dumber than a door knob," "cheap as dirt," "deaf as a mule," "drunk as a skunk," "blind as a bat," and "uglier than sin," to quote a few.

Cordell Richards remembered the two most frequently used terms were "deaf as Clem Pearce" and "much paint on him as William Smith."

These descriptions obviously referred to well-known gentlemen in the community. Clem, another local store proprietor, was very hard of hearing and conversation with him included repeat, repeat, repeat before he understood what you were saying. William was a skilled painter of houses and often wore to the store "evidence" of his trade.

Late one long summer afternoon, I silently slipped through the backdoor and comfortably settled in my favorite listening corner underneath Daddy's desk. The ring of the store phone interrupted my concentration. The rotary-dial telephone sat on a shelf directly across from where I was hiding. I jumped at the noise and then immediately froze in fear of being discovered by the person who would be approaching to answer that phone. After about five or six consecutive rings, my daddy spoke up.

"Leonard, you might as well go answer that aggravating phone. It's probably your sister-in-law calling to talk to you."

Like most of those who patronized this country store, Leonard did not have a telephone in his house. Family and friends who had phones and wished to get in contact with these men knew they could usually contact them if they called the store and asked to speak with them.

I heard Leonard's grumbling tone as he scuffed his feet and exited his heated conversation with his friends. He definitely wasn't eager to make his way back to that "cussed" phone. Fearing I was going to be discovered, I pressed closer to the backside underneath the desk and waited for Leonard to answer the phone.

Peering at me through a stack of papers at the far end underneath the desk was my trusted little mouse friend. He, too, obviously shared the fear of being discovered. We both remained frozen.

"Hello!"

Leonard answered the phone with an obvious tone of annoyance.

Managing to resist the urge to laugh aloud, I watched with amusement while Leonard stood holding that phone and shuffling his weight from one foot to the other. Occasionally he uttered a reluctant "Yeah" or "Okay."

In a phone call that lasted a good thirty minutes or more, Leonard was only afforded the opportunity to inject just those occasional comments. The entirety of the phone conversation was monopolized by the caller on the other end of the line. The lengthy phone call was an exhausting experience for not only Leonard but also for me and my little mouse friend. I have often wondered who was more worn out during that phone call. Was it me anxiously waiting while I endured the dust-ridden perch on the floor or Leonard as he became more impatient with each word coming through that telephone line into his exhausted ear?

Finally, after what seemed like an eternity, Leonard managed to say one uninterrupted word,

"Goodbye."

With this said, he replaced the phone. He returned to the front of the store and was greeted by ridiculing and laughing remarks about his not-so-short and one-sided-conversation.

I breathed a sigh of relief over not being discovered in my secret hiding place. Exhausted from my position of "freeze" during that long telephone exchange, I discreetly slipped out the back door and returned home.

Over the years, I encountered countless numbers of ease-dropping incidents under that desk. Daddy never called attention to my secret antics; but, I feel confident he was aware every time that I sneaked in his office and became entertained by his friends. Gone but not forgotten, these hidden away "country store collectibles" left lasting memories in my heart.

Chapter Twelve

SHARED JOYS OF YOUNG ADULTHOOD

Monday through Friday, for nine months out of the year, a few school-age patrons huddled together around the potbellied stove and awaited the arrival of their school bus.

Buses from two different school systems turned around at the store. The Murray family (JoAnn, Billie, Tony, Brenda and Vick), who had previously been enrolled in Rolesville school system, moved into an area designated as part of the Zebulon (Wakelon) school system. Each morning, they left their home and drove to the store where they parked their car and met the bus headed for Rolesville.

In addition to the Murrays, members of the Baker family (Rose, Louise, Pam and Joan) also met at the store to ride the Rolesville bus. They lived down a long path through the woods across from the store. Later, this Rolesville bound group was joined by Curtis Alford

School kids gather around the potbellied-stove

who had moved in with his Aunt Ruth after her husband, Leonard, died. He walked from her house to the store until she finally got her driver's license and drove him in her little Ford Falcon.

Some of the students who resided in Franklin County desired to attend school in Wake County. Their school of preference was part of the Zebulon (Wakelon) school system. In order to accomplish that feat, they met the school bus at the store. The Arnolds (Larry, Curt and

Brenda) drove to the store and left their parked car to board the bus. Another Franklin County family, the Jacksons (J.A. and Guy) were dropped off by their parents at the store so they could attend the school in Wake County.

Sometimes, Daddy would go after Floyd Gay to manage the store while he was away. Floyd's grandson, Richard Gay, would accompany them on the ride back to the store where he, another Franklin County resident, rode the bus to Wakelon. Richard and two of his cousins, Waddell Gay and Tim Gay, normally had to travel down to the end of their road to cross the Wake/Franklin County line and be permitted to attend Wakelon School.

Tony Murray attended Rolesville High School.

The final two students meeting the bus in route to Wakelon were me and Berry Privette. We only had to walk a few feet to accomplish this task.

Larry Arnold attended Wakelon High School

Randy Privette was not old enough to attend school; but, every afternoon just before the bus arrived he would cross the road, sit on one of the tobacco-warehouse benches under the store shelter, and anxiously await his older brother's return from school. With his little skinny legs swinging back and forth as he sat on the bench, he waited patiently. Finally, the bus drove up, the door swung open and Berry stepped out to be greeted by a big, missing-tooth smile on the face of his proud little brother.

If there were any sports or other form of rivalry between the two schools, it was never expressed among the members of this close-knit group. Sadly, though, tragedy struck members of this small group three different times before they completed their school years. February 28, 1956, Rose Baker, age 17, was killed in an automobile accident in which she was driving. February 26, 1957, Richard Gay, age 10, drowned in a small pond located behind the home of his grandparents with whom he resided. Then again on May 22, 1960 tragedy again happened. Curtis Arnold, age 16, was killed on Mitchell Mill Road in an automobile wreck in which he was a passenger. With each of these deaths, loss overwhelmed us because losing these individuals was like losing a close-family member.

Life moved on and the buses continued to come and go. It was common to see a large number of students step out of the bus when it stopped in front of the store. The Wakelon bus driver bribed his group into behaving while on his bus. The deal was, if they behaved, he would stop the bus for five minutes at O.B. Gay's store and allow them to run in and purchase candy or whatever. They always returned to the bus with their little brown bag filled with goodies and rode away "happy campers."

During the summer months, when there were no school buses running, the back yard of the store served as a playground for me, my cousins, and many of the neighborhood kids. From drawing a large circle on the ground and playing marbles to setting up a big hulled-out galvanized "wash tub" covered with a piece of chicken wire for roasting hot dogs, there was always something to do.

Seldom were there any girls who accompanied the dads to the country store. Only the boys came; therefore, to have them as playmates, I had to master the games the boys enjoyed to maintain a competitive standing.

When we had a larger group of kids gathered on the store grounds, we usually played games such as "Red Rover," "Simon Says," "Leap Frog," "Hopscotch," or "Hide and Seek." There was no lack of events to challenge our competitive skills.

A few of the kids loved to play "Jacks" where you bounced a little rubber ball into the air and scrambled to pick up all the little six-pointed jacks before the ball hit the ground. Some of us never became too involved in this game. We were more interested in "shooting" marbles.

These country boys were very competitive and they had no intention of letting me win just because I was a girl. Marbles was one of my favorite games. We would get down on the ground at the back of the store, draw a big circle and let the fun begin.

At the start of the game, each of us had a jar filled with colorful marbles crafted from glass. I had a few of the old clay marbles from the 1940s and earlier which I obtained from my Uncle Nig. Also, I had some "steel" marbles that my Uncle Davis brought me. These were discarded ball-bearings from equipment where he worked in Bailey.

Like the adults and their poker chips, we played "for keeps." We were "out for blood" and showed no mercy to our opponent in this game. Someone always left with more marbles in their jar than when they first arrived. Others left with fewer or no marbles at all. Whether it was skill or unyielding determination, I usually increased my marbles collection with each game we played.

Because of the numerous times we played this game, I found the fabric in my jeans shredded and I wore holes in the knee section.

"Who had time to worry about preserving jeans when knuckling down to an intensified game of marbles?"

That was the least of my concern. With a keen eye and a steady hand, we folded the palm of our hand and turned it upside-down leaving a spaced-out area where the thumb rested securely beneath the forefinger. Here we placed our chosen shooter marble. With a twist of the hand and a careful aim, the "shooter" was launched into the ring full of marbles. As a result, I often ended up with a rough, rounded-out-hole in the middle of the thumb nail on my right hand. After all, this was my "shooter" hand. (Like so many older adults who participated in any sports competition in their youth, now in my seventies, I find myself saddled with arthritis enveloping my marble "shooter" thumb).

Marble playing usually ended up with no fussing or fighting. However, tri-bike-riding was a little more intense, I was the proud owner of one of the few tri-bikes in the area. This bike was different from the average tricycle because the two rear wheels were larger. Naturally, this was one of the best means of entertainment for the boys, and I had no problem sharing with them, with one exception. When Jerry finished his "turn" riding the bike, he often refused to let it go. A big argument ensued, tempers flared and a fist fight erupted. He ran to the store and complained to his daddy who retorted,

"I can't believe you let a girl beat you up. Quit your whining and get back out there and play right."

Jerry returned, we patched things up and continued playing for hours.

Before summer vacation began, a salesman visited the school and promoted yo-yo competitive spirit. He gave demonstrations on the many ways to have fun with these little round toys. The yo-yos ranged from the regular wooden ones to the fancy and colorful. Kids learned many tricks from the salesman's instructions. With the onset of summer the neighborhood kids brought their school yard talents to the store. They would "show-off" their mastered skills of "going around the world," "walking the dog," "rocking the baby," "skinning the cat," and countless other accomplishments of the game. We had many hours of fun playing this game.

A few times I managed to convince a couple of the boys in the neighborhood to join me in a tea party in my playhouse out back of the store. That was only fair, right? They reluctantly complied; but, they made me promise never to tell their friends or anyone else that they had played girls' games. To that end, I will not reveal their names in this writing. If they read this book, I'm sure they will remember and know who I was talking about.

Most of my sports participation was not with the neighborhood boys but with my daddy. He would convince my mother to attend to the store while he gathered up a baseball or softball, a bat and a couple of ball gloves. We played many hours of catch and hitting fly balls; but. he was not interested in playing badminton. However, two young boys in the community, Randy Privette and Craig Mullins, were eager to learn and play the game. We set up the metal poles, stretched the net across from one end to the other, grabbed our rackets and pounded away at that flimsy "birdie." Those little fellows had more energy than I could handle; but we had countless hours of fun playing and laughing at our mistakes.

In the summer months during the 1970s, my Godson, Scott "Bubba" Johnston along with his brother, Adam Johnston, became delighted for the opportunity to escape the city life and spend time roaming the wide-open spaces found on the farm. Additionally, they eagerly entered the country store and embraced the readily-available goodies awaiting them. Both boys shared an enthusiasm for the in-store special treatment they received. Of the two, Bubba was more inquisitive. He not only was my daddy's Godson, but he became his "side-kick" when he visited the country. He and Adam loved to ride with Daddy when he took time off from the store and went fishing in the Gay family's ten-acre pond in Franklin County.

When they returned to the store, Bubba watched with intensity while Daddy removed the "catches of the day" from the galvanized pail and prepared them for human consumption later in the evening. He had encouraged the boys to place their catch into the pail even though the fish may not have been large enough to eat. These smaller fish were placed in a plastic bucket filled with water. Then he and the boys transported these fish to a "water hole" on the farm. They released them into the water with the anticipation these little fish would have time to grow larger before anyone caught them at the end of their fishing line.

Bubba, who today is an avid collector of older guns, conceivably could have acquired his appreciation of fire arms while visiting the country store. Daddy led him into the side room of the store and taught him how to fire his nine-shot 22 caliber pistol. His target practice consisted of ridding the premises of those pesky rodents. Bubba took aim and fired at the scurrying rats as they attempted to escape from underneath the bags of fertilizer and seeds where they were residing. Safety in proper gun-handling was emphasized and a "no-tell" agreement bound them in secrecy.

Whether the youth who entered Daddy's store became my playmates, became a "sidekick" for Daddy or simply walked away with a bag of candy secretly given to them by Daddy, they each carried with them fond memories of the old country store.

Chapter Thirteen

RERUNS & RECYCLES ABOUND

Today, familiarity with reruns on television is universal. Prior to the 1950s, television show reruns were nonexistent because a television program had to first be recorded on film to become a rerun. Television shows were aired live and once they were aired they became history. Thus, with the implementation of film recording, television programs airing more than one time following their initial broadcast were referred to as "reruns." Some viewers welcomed the opportunity to watch these shows over and over. Others felt reruns were an absolute nuisance.

Daddy concurred with the absolute nuisance conclusion and further argued that the emergence of "reruns" was not something new. According to him, the originality of these phenomena materialized prior to the introduction via television; and, he felt the country store "stage" was the forerunner of television reruns. He continued,

"Day after day, I listened to reruns when someone would come into the store and talk about planting, 'putting-in' or selling tobacco. Once one person left the store, another would enter and I was forced to listen to a repeat of the same story."

From one customer to the next, same stories were "rerun" for the listening ear. Reruns were a common, everyday addition to the conversations of the country store patrons.

With a sly chuckle, Daddy afforded another example of the reruns he endured:

"The next month someone might come in with a story about hunting or fishing, about who killed the largest covey of birds or who caught the biggest fish. Once again, the story became a rerun when it was repeated to the next customer that stepped through the door."

These reruns tended to differ from television reruns in that the repeated stories of the patrons often contained added information with each subsequent rendering. Reruns of this era would someday be fondly referred to as "Country Store Collectibles" of American History.

"Recycling," according to Daddy, was nothing new either. He explained that the process of recycling was practiced in the country store and rural households long before it became an environmental issue.

The fundamental theory of economics concerning supply and demand played a significant role in the practice of recycling.

Decades before the recycling process was viewed as fashionable, many items sold in O.B. Gay's store were deemed reusable. Household recycling was a common practice because often it was monetarily more practical to reuse some items rather than purchase new ones. Plain or picturesque jelly jars were used as drinking glasses after the contents of the jar had been consumed. Empty coffee cans were used to collect fresh worms for the next fishing expedition. Empty cigar boxes were used to conceal prized collections or to store important papers. Wooden cheese boxes, once emptied and wiped clean to remove the strong smell, were used for nesting hens, women's hat boxes and a variety of other uses. Some of the empty cheese boxes were filled with dirt and used at the base of the potbellied stove to collect spit from tobacco chewers and snuff dippers. They were emptied daily, refilled with dirt, and reused the next day. This recycling process was repeated until the sturdiness of the box itself became an issue.

Feed sacks became one of the most recyclable items of all time from the 1930s through the 1950s. Local women reused the original plain white cotton sacks in their kitchen for dish towels and tablecloths. A few of the ladies even used these white sacks to make underwear for their children and sometimes for their husband or for their own use. Before any of these sacks were converted into wearable clothing, they underwent numerous washes to cleanse the material, especially those sacks chosen to be used as diapers for their infants.

As time went on, feed sacks came in a variety of colors and some even had embodied prints. The practice of making nice pretty dresses or dressy print shirts from these emptied and washed feed sacks became commonplace in almost every home in our community. It was not unusual for the women to accompany their husbands to the store just to make sure the feed they purchased was in a specific color or pattern. The women browsed through sacks of grain-filled bags before they chose the exact print to meet the recycled needs of their future sewing endeavors. Sturdy, pretty, flowered fabrics were the best sellers. Sometimes, the dresses made from this material could be recycled again once the person wearing the dress had outgrown it. Once the dress could no longer be worn by a member of the family, the material would be washed and cut into small pieces. The pieces were arranged in a pattern, sewed together, and eventually became part of a multi-colored quilt for some lucky recipient's warm covering on a cold wintery night.

Next, soda bottle caps became an increasingly sought-after recyclable item. These crown caps were filled with a cork lining in the

1940s and 1950s. Beginning in the 1960s, cork became more expensive. Subsequently, manufacturers replaced them with plastic as a liner for the bottle caps.

Bottle caps were removed with the use of a bottle opener. There were two openers and each was located at opposite ends on the front of the chest-like drink box in O.B. Gay's store. Immediately beneath these metal bottle openers was a slot-like collection tray for the caps once they were pried off the drink bottle. Daddy remembered,

"I kept a two-gallon bucket underneath my sales counter. Each night before I closed the store, I would remove the tray filled with bottle caps from the drink box and empty them into that bucket."

Each spring or early summer, just prior to tobacco harvesting time, the farmers gathered the thick guano sacks they had saved after emptying the fertilizer from them. These sacks would be recycled and used as side curtains to prevent tobacco leaf spillage on the slide truck that transported tobacco from field to barn. To prepare for this feat, farmers visited the local general store to obtain the necessary items.

"Oris, did you save any bottle caps this year? It's time to replace the side sheets on my tobacco trucks and I need a bunch of bottle caps."

"Yeah, I knew you boys would be coming by soon. Grab a paper bag from under the counter and fill it up with bottle caps from that bucket beside the storage room door. The bucket is full so help yourself."

The farmers filled their bags and were on their way. Once they had their tobacco truck slides in place, they nailed the bottle caps along the top of the rails to form a snug fit and secure the sacks in place.

Furnishing these bottle caps for the farmers to recycle was just one more way Daddy extended special service to the friends and neighbors in his country store community.

Chapter Fourteen

VOLUNTEERS TO THE RESCUE

The fall and winter of 1954 entered and exited leaving in their path a devastating reminder of Hurricane Hazel. Only a year earlier, the yard surrounding our home and country store was shaded by full-branch, aged oak trees that proudly stood tall and weathered countless storms. The area where those trees once stood was replaced by huge dirt-filled holes resulting from the upheaval left by the hurricane. As a safety precaution, area children and adults gathered in the store and watched out the front windows while Hazel's wrath uprooted a big tree and landed in on the home of Mr. Willie and Mrs. Maude Privette. That was a scary time and we felt the only sturdy structure was the store building. When the storm subsided and we exited the store, we were confronted with a scene reflective of a war zone. That old country store was truly our haven of rescue.

With the onset of a new year came hope and anticipation of better things to come. New beginnings abounded once February approached and the postal delivery truck arrived with precious cargo. The baby chickens Mother mail-ordered were finally here. Overwhelmed with excitement and curiosity, I gleefully tugged at Mother's apron.

"What is it? Can I please see?" I questioned.

She replied,

"These are baby chickens. We call them 'biddies.' Because we don't have their small stick-built pens ready for them, we are going to place them in incubators until the weather becomes warmer. You can watch them grow."

"Will they become full grown chickens like the ones we have running around the yard? I'm sure glad you didn't order any more guineas. I hate guineas! I can't even walk outside without being chased all over the yard by them. They will not leave you alone until they have pecked your skin enough to draw blood. Can I just keep the biddies for my pets and never let them grow up to be yucky old chickens?"

She smiled and reminded me,

"Farm animals are not pets. Don't get too attached. Just think, you can still watch them grow and you can be the one that takes special care of them while they are babies. Caring for these biddies can be your responsibility, if you choose to watch over them. It will be up to you to take good care of them by making sure they are fed and watered, and are safe."

Ecstatically, I eagerly agreed to assume full responsibility and promised,

"I will watch over them every day."

Weeks later, on a beautiful spring morning, I strolled along the path from our house to the store. I became acutely aware of the pleasantness that surrounded me. The newly planted oak trees were making their entry onto the scene. Pink and white buds were forming on the fruit trees. Floral blooms would soon travel along the thin tree limbs and by summer a harvest of either apples, pears or peaches would be ready for consumption. In long rows behind the fruit trees, the seeds we planted in early November of the previous year now sprouted and burst through the ground. An array of bright and colorful flowers provided a vivid display of beauty along the pathway.

Scuffling noise, accompanied by soft chirping, permeated from the incubators in the chicken house. I opened the door and peered at them and was quickly overcome with laughter and glee. Their sweet sounds filled the air with the gentleness of music.

Approaching the tobacco barn located midway along the store path, I witnessed playful activity coming from one of the barn shelters. Newborn puppies were frolicking and barking while they attempted to stand and take their first steps. I chuckled when they almost came to a complete stand only to lose their balance and fall on their face. They remained persistent and determined to accomplish their task.

I called out to our beautiful brown and white setter birddog,

"Great job Lou! You make a good mother for your pups. Six of the prettiest little puppies I've ever seen. I sure wish I could play with them but Daddy would be very angry."

Daddy wanted these puppies to grow up and be trained for quail hunting. His goal was to have the best "pointer" and "setter" birddogs with the onset of hunting season in the fall.

Lou raised her weary head and looked at me implying she understood every word. Despite Daddy's warnings, I still managed to persuade him to relinquish one of the pups which he determined would never make a good birddog.

"You really don't like that puppy, do you? Is it because he has a round circle around one eye; or, is it because he is solid white except for a little brown hair on the tip of his tail?"

Daddy just stood there and looked at me. He glanced down at the puppy and then back at me. Maybe this was my chance.

"Since that's never going to be one of your hunting dogs, may I please have him as a pet?"

Daddy mumbled back,

"Go ahead. You can have him. Dog liters are just like cars. There's always one lemon in the group."

"Lemon, that's a good name for him, Daddy. He may look like a 'lemon' to you; but, his yellowish eye with the black circle around it looks like a fresh lemon citrus fruit to me."

Daddy and I both burst into laughter. For many seasons, Lemon and I had hours of fun and pleasure romping across the yard and the adjacent tobacco and grain fields.

Continuing along the path to the store, I paused to watch small kittens as they scampered about and chased each other. Next, they jumped into the air when bugs, butterflies, and sometimes birds flew above their head. Being a dog lover at that time, cats were not at all appealing to me. Their main purpose was to cut down on the rat population occupying the farm buildings. A couple of the "fat" cats camped-out underneath the store and engaged in the elimination process of the rats. These rats resided beneath the floor space that housed fertilizer and seeds.

Once past the barn, in the distance I heard a rooster crowing loudly. Cautiously, I approached hoping the sound was not from Mother's little bantam rooster. I hated that rooster with its puffed-up feathers. He possessed the most aggressive disposition of any of our farm animals. The other animals also expressed animosity toward him. Cats and dogs loved to chase him and he was "lunch" for the stalking hawk.

"Cock-a-doodle-do!" Good morning to you!

This message, to my relief, radiated from one of the larger, and friendlier roosters. Perched upright on a tree log, the proud rooster spread his wings and looked out over his feather-strutting hens. They repeatedly clucked and completely ignored him. Guess he wasn't the "cock of the walk" that day!

I stopped and gazed at those hens. I was almost certain some of them were the culprits who had pecked the heck out of my hand last evening when I attempted to gather eggs from beneath them as they sat on their nest. I thought,

"Let those aggravating hens strut and cluck to their heart's desire. Stay in the field and don't come near me. Everything will be just fine if they don't walk down the store path and leave little deposits to get stuck between the toes of my bare feet. Yuk!"

Enjoying the pleasant smell of flowers and budding trees, I continued my walk. There was a new smell in the air. The sweetest aroma was drifting from the wood-burning stove in Mother's kitchen. She had recently removed from the oven a nice, juicy banana pudding topped off with swirling layers of lightly browned moraine. My taste buds swelled with anticipation and I envisioned a bowl filled with heavenly delight.

When I approached the back door of the store, an entirely different smell crossed my nose. It came from a galvanized bucket filled with fresh-water fish. Daddy had returned from a local pond. He placed his catch-of-the-day on the trusty scales while two of his customers waited for the calculation.

Since Daddy had returned that meant Mother was free to accompany me to the house. That was an encouraging sign for me.

With a sneaky smile on my face, I slowly approached her and whispered,

"Mother, you know you want to go to the house with me!"

She gave me a questioning look.

"What are you up to? You want something and I have a good idea what it is."

She added,

"Don't even ask! You know that banana pudding must cool off before it can be served. Besides, it is for supper, not snack time!"

After what seemed like the longest hesitation ever, she glanced at Daddy and winked. She turned and walked out the back door of the store. Looking back over her shoulder, she called to me,

"Well, okay but we need to hurry. It's almost time for me to start supper. I need to get back to the store afterwards so your daddy can go eat."

Following Mother to the house, I exerted every effort to keep in step with her fast pace. Suddenly, I felt an eerie sense of uneasiness. An unexplainable urgency caused me to pause along the way and call out to Mother,

"Go ahead and fix us a bowl of that delicious pudding. Give me just a minute. I really need to check on my little biddies!"

By this time, her patience with me was growing thin. She gave me a disapproving glance, turned, and hurried on her way. I pretended not to notice her frustration and started running across the path.

I approached the biddies' house and hesitated at the door. Some disturbing noises came from inside. The usually happy chirping was being replaced by scream-like choking sounds.

I immediately flung the door open and stepped back in shock. The entire room became completely engulfed in smoke. I listened as frightened little biddies moved about and made high-pitched, frantic sounds. The thickness of smoke made locating the biddies virtually impossible. A corner in the back was the most smoke-concentrated section of the room. Panic consumed me when I realized an object that resembled a spark was evolving into a small flame.

Overwhelmed with fear, my heart raced and my brain screamed. I struggled to yell for help but was unable to speak above a whisper. I exited the door and ran back to the store. Gasping for breath, and with tears flooding my heated cheeks, I almost fell forward while climbing the steps. I burst through the back door and somehow managed to plead with the men gathered in the store.

"Please help me! Get some water quick!"

At first the men just stared at me with a puzzled look on their faces. I had interrupted their fish-tales swap with my frantic blabbering.

I continued to scream at them,

"There is a fire inside the house where the biddies are. Those poor little darlings are going to burn to death if you don't hurry!"

The men, realizing I was serious wasted no time in responding. They quickly jumped to their feet. Freddie grabbed a long water hose from the store shelf and joined the others as they raced toward the smoke-filled building. When they reached their destination, he threw the hose on the ground and yelled,

"Add this water hose to the one already hooked up the water spigot."

Fortunately, the outdoor faucet was adjacent to the little building and only about twenty feet away. Grover was the first man to reach the building. He carefully opened the door, peered in, and yelled back to the men gathered outside,

"You need to tighten the nozzle on that hose and get it to me. Get some water in here quick!"

Aubrey and Ned tried to untangle the wound-up water hose and stretch it out. Daddy and his brother, A.O., grabbed the hose and kept pushing forward. The "rescuers" entered the building and extinguished the blazed area.

Everything progressed systematically. Those wonderful volunteers diligently worked in a collective effort to assure the successful rescue of little lives on that frightful day. Throughout the entire ordeal, I continued to scream my concerns.

"Hurry, please hurry! Please don't let them die!"

Once the fire was contained and the smoke cleared, it was discovered that the wiring from a light in the incubator had frayed. Subsequently, the result was a burst of flames. After the flames were extinguished, the fire-damaged incubator was removed from the building and tossed aside.

I cautiously approached the watered-down, smoke-cleared building and walked from one biddy to another to reaffirm they were still alive. My attention was drawn to the group of little biddies that had been trapped in the damaged incubator. I began to cry. Their beautiful little yellow-feathered bodies were covered in watered-down soot. Two of them lay motionless on the floor.

"Oh no! These two little ones didn't make it," I exclaimed.

Sadness enveloped me. I bent down and picked up their motionless limp bodies. Mother walked up and stood beside me. I wanted to run to her and receive comforting; instead, I gently passed the little ones over to her for disposal. She cupped them in the palm of her hand and carried them outside to be buried. Moments later, happy sounds of laughter could be heard coming from a side window of the building. I rushed over to the window and Mother held the chicks high. A frail chirping sound became audibly clear. Filled with optimistic excitement, I ran outside.

"Is it true? Are they breathing?"

Mother nodded her head up and down. She looked at me and smiled as I continued to rattle on.

"Did I really hear them chirping or was I dreaming? They are alive, aren't they? Mother, please tell me they are going to be alright!"

She gave me a look of reassurance. My wonderful mother turned to me and smiled. With utmost care and concern, she placed two squirming little biddies into my outstretched arms. With a big smile on her face, she continued,

"Yes, they are going to be okay. They just needed some fresh air to clear the smoke which they inhaled. Go ahead, rub their little heads. And for goodness sake, stop that crying."

To my astonishment and delight, the lives of all those biddies were spared thanks to God for answered prayers and to the collective efforts of those wonderful friends and neighbors. They willingly responded to my pleas for help. They valiantly plunged through the smoke, extinguished the fire, and returned calmness to a potentially chaotic situation.

Finally, feeling relieved and extremely thankful, I could enjoy Mother's banana pudding. In fact, we carried the entire bowl of pudding to the store and shared with our "heroes" of the day – those wonderful country store patrons.

This entire incident was so typical of the way local people in our community, especially those men who frequented Daddy's store, came together in time of need and never complained when someone (even if it was just a kid) requested their assistance.

As fate would have it, this was not the only occasion I found myself forced to enlist help from individuals gathered together at Daddy's store. I recall an incident that took place in the summer of 1966. And once again, smoke was the culprit!

I awakened to the sound of a pickup truck horn blowing non-stop. I raised the window shade in my bedroom and peered out at the parked truck on the road in front of our house. Some stranger waved his hands in the air and pointed to the top of our house. I opened the front door and asked,

"What's with all that horn blowing and yelling? And why are you waving your arms and pointing at our house?"

He screamed back in a voice that, by this time, was beginning to crack and make his words hard to understand.

"Your house is on fire! You need to get out! Smoke is coming from your attic and pouring out the window over your front porch!"

Heavy foot-pounding sounds erupted and several men rushed across our front porch. Added to this commotion was the sound of loud and erratic talking. They quickly gained my attention.

One excited, but commanding, voice filled with urgency resounded above all the talking. I recognized, at once, that this was my cousin Aubrey.

"Grab a ladder and run it up to that window on top of the porch! Come on boys, get the lead out! Hustle!"

I put on my shoes and unlocked and opened the front door to enable the men to enter the house. I called out to Mother who was asleep in the room down the hall from my bedroom.

"Mother, you need to get up real quick. We have to get out of here. Our house is on fire!"

Startled at my outcry, she sat up in bed, threw back the coverings and stared at me with a puzzled look. I ran to the kitchen, grabbed my car keys from the wall hanger, and fled out the back door.

Once outside, I rolled the top down on my 1966 Chevy convertible and backed the car near the rear steps to our house. Wasting no time, I reentered the house, ran to my bedroom, grabbed two clothes-filled dresser drawers, and headed back to my car. When I passed through my parents' bedroom, I found Mother standing beside her bed. She was still in her nightgown, motionless.

"Mother, did you hear what I said to you. You really need to get dressed and get out of here. I'm trying to get a few of my things so they won't be burned up in the fire."

Yet, she remained completely oblivious to the dramatic scene that was unfolding all around her.

I ran back into the house and grabbed two more dresser drawers. All I could think about was,

"Even if the house burns down, at least I will have some clothes to wear."

I paused for a moment as I once again ran through Mother's bedroom. She was still standing beside her bed. She looked at me like I had completely lost my mind.

"What are you doing," she inquired.

Obviously flabbergasted, she continued,

"Are you having a bad dream or have you gone crazy. I don't see any fire."

I turned to her and replied,

"All I know is some man blew his truck horn and another man pounded on my front door and yelled 'fire.' He didn't have to tell me twice. I hauled tail! You need to get dressed and get out of here now!"

I made a few more trips back into the house to gather clothing, record collections, and other cherished items. I continued to pass by Mother while she attempted to change her clothing. By the time she finished dressing, I had filled my car with items deemed valuable to me. Looking back, I was relieved to see Mother had finally exited the house and was on her way to the store. I drove my "treasure-filled" car to the store and sighed a breath of exhausted relief.

Once out of my car, I heard laughter coming from within the store. In my haste to gather my belongings, I failed to recognize that the men had extinguished the potential fire hazard and returned to the store. The small electrical spark igniting from a frayed wire had been corrected and the smoke had receded. The men watched with amusement as I repeatedly returned to my car with another armful of my possessions.

During the weeks that followed, I was subjected to joking remarks relative to this dramatic event. Even my mother, who throughout the entire ordeal remained in a fixed position, afforded teasing jests. Appraising the whole situation, I, too, recognized the comedic appearance and welcomed their joking remarks.

Once again "country folks" rushed to the rescue whenever a need presented itself. There were no people in the world more loyal and dependable than the country-store-patrons at O.B. Gay's store. God bless them all.

Some of the young men who were so instrumental in the late 1950's and 1960's fire prevention episodes above later became volunteers and members of the Hopkins Rural Fire Department established in the late 1970's. Perhaps their previous fire-fighting experiences provided the enthusiasm needed to prepare them for their volunteer services to the community.

Chapter Fifteen

A HAVEN FROM STORMS

October 15, 1954, we were out of school because a severe storm was approaching. Some kids and adults were at the store. We all gathered there because we felt that building was much sturdier than our house or any of the other buildings located on the property.

There were a few people in the "strip room" where they were sorting and tying up bundles of tobacco in preparation for delivery to the tobacco market. As weather conditions worsened, those people emerged from where they were working and joined the rest of us who were huddled together in the store.

We watched intently from the heavy, barred windows on the front of the store. Suddenly, we witnessed a large oak tree being pulled up by its ground roots; it toppled on the roof of Willie and Maude Privette's house. We feared for their safety.

Winds whistled outside and the tin top on the store continued to rumble. Small tree limbs and debris steadily blew underneath the store shelter.

Prior to the storm, Daddy pulled the outside door shut over the window on the side of the store. That boarded-up window withstood a tremendous pounding from the storm but remained secure. The sturdy A-framed store building provided a stable fortress for the ones huddled inside.

We continued to hear the wind roar in the distance. Trees crackled and crashed to the ground. We watched as they fell in the surrounding wooded areas. Then we heard the crushing sounds while other trees fell atop the outside buildings in their pathway.

We anxiously waited, never knowing if the rumbling tin would be ripped off the top of the store at any moment. We feared the roof would open and reveal an angry sky filled with the frightening sight of flying objects. We kids were unaware there was an attic to the store and that the possibility of objects being flung from the store into the air was highly unlikely.

We listened intently to the adults as they voiced their concerns of what could be happening to our house and the outside buildings as well as the homes of others in the community. The adults wondered aloud,

"Will we be faced with the devastation of flattened homes and scattered possessions?"

We continued to remain inside the store until the winds subsided and the men determined the powerful hurricane had passed.

Once it was over, Daddy opened the boarded-up side window of the store and looked outside. Then he opened the back doors and stepped outside to assess the devastation "Hurricane Hazel" left behind.

Trees lay flat on the ground and debris covered almost every inch of the yard. There was a toppled tree on our house. Side boards and barn tops were ripped and the roofs of the storage houses were twisted and in shambles. The animals, thank the Lord, remained safe, but they were still in a state of panic as they wildly ran about the yard.

By the Grace of God, we were all safe and unharmed. The house and buildings were repairable. Once again, the old country store became a gathering place; this time, though, it became a "safe haven" for those gathered to escape the ravishing destruction outside the building.

Because of Hurricane Hazel's destructiveness, we lost electric power for days. Kerosene "hurricane" lamps were in demand. Fortunately, Daddy had stocked his store with lamp supplies to meet the needs of his customers. Kerosene, matches and wicks were available for them. Wicks for the lamps came in large round rolls. Strips from these rolls were cut off and sold to be used in the hurricane lamps. Kerosene was placed in the bottom of the lamps and the wicks were adjusted to absorb enough of the liquid to enable it to ignite once the match was struck and placed next to the soaked wick. The globe was then placed on the lamps and lanterns. The ignited wick was turned up to reveal a light that was bright enough to illuminate the room.

This method of lighting is still practiced today by some when storms or accidents result in an electrical power outage. For those of us who weathered those storms of yesteryear, these hurricane lamps, in addition to room illumination, provide us a nostalgic step down memory lane. They remind us there are still simple ways to meet a crisis.

Chapter Sixteen

VALUABLE IN-STORE EDUCATION

My parents were reared on the farm and the opportunity to attend school and receive an education was interrupted. My daddy completed the fifth grade and my mother completed the eighth grade. Each of them was forced to discontinue their education to perform the necessary tasks needed to assist their parents in their home and farm. Families throughout the rural area were faced with this dilemma. Daddy and his oldest brothers managed the farm operations. Mother, at age four, was placed on a small stool where she began her infamous reputation of being the best homemade biscuit maker around (long before the fast food exchange, Hardees, claimed this title). Mother and her sister, Bet, being the two oldest of seven children, became caregivers for their siblings and responsible for their farm chores.

Harboring a sense of inadequacy over their incomplete education, my parents were adamant that I be afforded attainment of a formal education. They never had to persuade me to go to school. I attended Wakelon School in Zebuon for all twelve years and never missed a day. If the school bus left without me, I would cry until Daddy drove me to school. Mother even sent me to school when I had the mumps in the tenth grade. She coated my under chin and neck area with sardine oil and wrapped a scarf around it to disguise the swelling; however, there was no disguising that smell. I encountered several "get away from me" glances from my friends and fellow students.

From over in the corner of the room during our Friday morning Latin class, I heard someone say,

"What is that awful smell?"

Our teacher, Mr. Ussery, went over and spoke with the boy who had asked the question. Then he returned to his desk and instructed us to write down all the information he had printed on the blackboard. While everyone was busy writing, he came by my desk and asked me to join him in the hallway. He began speaking,

"Miss, you need to go to the office and telephone your parents and ask them to come and pick you up from school."

With my onset of mumps and the swelling of my glands, my frantic attempt to speak resulted in a mumble,

"But Mr. Ussery, I just can't do that! This is my tenth year with perfect attendance. If I have to leave school now and go home I will lose my perfect attendance record!"

He reassured me,

"Your perfect attendance record will not be jeopardized. You will receive full credit for attending school today since it is past eleven o'clock. The swelling will probably only last a total of three days. By Monday your swelling should be gone and you can return to school and still not miss a day."

He was so tactful and never referred to the atrocious smell and I never knew if anyone actually knew that I had the mumps. One factor remains evident, my classmates probably felt relieved when I exited the classroom.

Summers were busy working on the farm and in the store. However, I was still bored with no educational challenges during those months. Here's where the in-store education was introduced to me.

Daddy at 10-key adding machine

Daddy owned a gray ten-key manually operated adding machine which allowed entries of up to seven digit totals. Numbers were entered by depressing the keys and then pulling down on the crank on the right side of the machine. The number would print and the roll of adding machine tape would move forward. This antique method of machine adding has become obsolete today with the onslaught of decades of technological growth and improvement. From the manual keyboard adding machines to the introduction of electric operation, these machines have decreased in size and evolved into the fast-paced calculators conveniently held and operated in the palm of today's students and adults.

Math was Daddy's passion. From the days of his childhood, his brother, Leonard, would coax him into doing math homework for him; thus, he had a competitive edge on the subject. He introduced me to the absolute joy of making math fun during the summer months when school was out. When there were only one or two customers hanging out in the store, he would motion for one of the men to come over to the checkout counter.

"Take this piece of paper. I have written down several rows of numbers. Pick out one row and quickly call them out to me and Brenda."

Most of these numbers were usually double digits. Daddy would have a blank piece of paper and a pencil at his disposal. He placed me in front of the crank-handle adding machine and challenged me to a duel.

"Listen to the numbers being called out. I will add them on this piece of paper and you add them on the machine. Let's see who can get the answer the fastest. The fastest adder with the correct total will be the winner."

The customer would then call out, "ready, set, go!" and then proceed with the numbers. After adding two or three rows of numbers, we would switch positions with him on the machine and me on the paper. Not only was the challenge of the game entertaining; but, the enthusiasm associated with this math instilled within me a desire to learn more. The many hours spent with my daddy and that little gray metal box with its sturdy handle (which amazingly remained intact despite the sometimes vigorously rough treatment inflicted upon it) left memories cherished forever. Even now, my granddaughters, neither of whom has a fondness for math, love to challenge this old white-headed granny in her seventies with math problems from their school assignments. Time after time, they look up from the paper on which they so rigorously attempt to arrive at the answer and shake their head in disbelief that Granny has already reached an answer. Often, they will challenge me with additional problems and use their calculators to declare victory. My track record against the calculator is not quite as fast as the old adding machine competition, but neither is it a total wash out. Thanks Daddy, I guess I haven't completely lost the skills you taught me.

Mother literally despised math and had little interest in attempting to use the old trusty adding machine. Casting math aside, she was an amazing source of reference when approached about the subject of English. She possessed an uncanny fascination with English grammar. Not unlike her love for jigsaw puzzles with the challenge to choose the exact puzzle piece to complete a full picture, her careful placement of the correct grammatical word was implemented to complete the perfect sentence. She often encouraged me to join her on the elongated bench behind the potbellied stove.

With outstretched legs, I leaned back on the bench and awaited her latest session on English grammar. Like Daddy's math teachings, Mother's English teachings, too, became the time for fun and learning. From verb conjugations to the differences between adverbs and adjectives, nouns and verbs, and when to use a pronoun instead of a noun, she always made learning an adventure. On several occasions, once a customer exited the store, she (with no degradation intended for that individual) would call my attention to a certain statement that customer had made.

"You got any Lucky Strikes?"

"It shore is hot out today, ain't it?"

"Gimme a sack of candy for the youngins."

Obediently, I wrote the words out as stated by the customer and inserted the grammatically correct words in their place to satisfy Mother's obsession with accuracy. I had little problem making the necessary adjustments on paper; however, when it came to verbal communication with others in our rural community, local terminology became my expression of choice. Use of the all-too-familiar terms (inaccurate though they were) allowed me to "fit in." After all, Mother wasn't listening and what good was it to be constantly focusing on word usage when engaging in friendly conversations with my friends and neighbors. Being an only child oftentimes made me the recipient of throw-off remarks from others. Why should I allow the title of grammar fanatic to become another encouraging "la-de-da" criticism?

Some other customers had a better command of the English language but chose to use slang just to see her cringe at the misuse of grammar.

"Whatcha got for this here sore throat?"

"I seen him in here yistidy and he want looking too good."

Just a few of the quoted statements above would be enough to get Mother's feathers riled. She challenged me to analyze the contents of their statements and grammatically correct the wording.

These words quoted herein are in no way intended to imply ignorance or lack of education. In one sense their command of the English language was commendable in that they could speak several sentences without even once inserting words of profanity or swearing. So often, today, that is a compromising challenge afforded even the best educated. In retrospect, I wonder if the reason Mother and I were not subjected to the unwelcomed words was because Daddy absolutely would not allow "such talk" when ladies were present. The one time I heard someone use curse words, I turned to see my daddy's face turn bright red. He came around from behind the counter and grabbed the man in his collar. Then he proceeded to turn the man around, marched him to the front door, and presented him with a foot-in-the-butt exit from the store.

Because of my parents' teachings, my passion for both math and English culminated into a union considered by others as an unusual, if not rare, combination. Most people I encountered either liked one or the other of these subjects but seldom had a preferred interest in the pairing of the two. I credit Daddy for introducing me to a subject that would later lead me into my occupational career in the accounting and tax preparation field. I credit Mother for introducing me to a subject that would not only aid me in my customer service employment but also allow me to enjoy my pastime endeavor of writing. Alas, I look back and yearn for the days of simple teachings that I received within the secure walls of our beloved country store. Education wise, this country girl had the better of two worlds.

Not only did I receive non-formal education from my parents but also from our diversified store patrons. Aside from watching Mr. Zollie Pearce practice his art of whittling and from listening to men tell how they caught fish and hunted prey, I enjoyed those individuals who ventured from the familiar farming activities and worked in other professions.

Returning veterans from World War II and other wars shared their military experiences and told of places they visited and some of the unusual customs of the other countries. Two of these men were Louis "Jack" Lloyd, who served with the U.S. Merchant Marines, and Jarvis "Jabo" Gay who served with the U.S. Navy. Stories they recounted were fascinating to me. Undoubtedly this was information that had been recorded by others in our school history books. However, listening to these men tell of their personal experiences as American military soldiers fighting wars in foreign countries resonated with me far more than that boring history lesson at school. Again, what better place to receive this education than in the old country store!

I learned lessons relative to banking along with money variations and stock values, vehicle repairs and maintenance, firsthand discoveries from world travelers, extracting metal from the rock quarry, crop planting and harvesting, flower planting, and food growing. These were some more of the "in-store" educational benefits I was privileged to experience.

Twelve years of traditional school never provided me the advantageous education afforded me in that old country store. An age old adage "common sense" is more beneficial than "book sense" bears much truth. Fortunately, I was blessed to have received just a touch of each.

In-store education continued to materialize in many forms. In the next section, I will introduce you to more customers who patronized O.B. Gay's store. You will probably recognize some similarity among these individuals; but their uniqueness of character separated them from the norm.

Individual traits of these patrons were readily identifiable. Some possessed the ability to openly vocalize their opinions. Others captured the attention of their audience by displaying their creativity with homespun tall tales.

Whether these men were engrossed in a card game, shooting a game of pool, or relaxing around the stove, laughter and lies normally filled the walls of the old country store.

Gone are the carefree moments of yesterday when I spent countless hours in the security of daddy's country store. I reflect fondly on the shared love between my parents and their sometimes-playful antics when the store wasn't full of customers. Etched permanently within the scope of my mind are those individuals that were such an intricate part of my childhood growing up in and around the store. There were so many different and unique personalities to choose from but only a small space to write about; therefore, a random selection was chosen to present herein.

Mischievous Oris with arm around Ruby

Chapter Seventeen

THE BAKERS DOZEN

(Not Doughnuts but 13 Delightful Patrons)

Those neighborhood men who patronized Daddy's store brought vibrant life as they escaped the trials of everyday work on the farm and gathered together for an evening of fun and relaxation. This group left behind a picturesque collection of country store memories.

Many times, the store was filled with men who were all in the same family. Mr. Charlie Baker's family: Horace, Charlie Dee, Grover, Freddie, Monroe, and Rudolph came almost every day. Other families who patronized the store almost daily were the Privettes (Donald, W.B., and Pete.) Their brothers, Millard, Perry, and Lewis, moved out the area, but frequented the store when visiting their parents. Other families included the Richards (Roscoe, Antrim, and Darnell), the Murrays (Adrian, Charlie, Millard, Robert), the Carters (Early and Demp), the Perrys (Byrd, Sun, Furney and many more), the Pearces (Arthur and countless others) the Wrights (Junior, Alvin and brothers), the Mitchells (Roy, Durwood and Buddy), the Dukes (Millard, Wayne, and Mayon) and neighbors, Claude and Mary Horton.

Mary and Claude Horton

There were numerous other families not included in this list of wonderful customers who made up the legacy of country store patrons.

Freddie Baker

Darnell Richards

I have selected only thirteen ("The Bakers Dozen") of those individuals who were valued customers at O.B. Gay's store. They possessed varied characteristics that left an impression for my picturesque presentation of the "norm." However, in retrospect, I soon realized there was no "norm" for those colorful individuals. While each customer shared a common bond of enjoying the fellowship they shared at the country store, they were alike; yet, they were also very different. Each of these men had a unique trait even amid the common bond that caused them to "stand-out" from the crowd.

With that said, let me begin by introducing one man who made an impact on the conversations shared in every country store he patronized.

(1)
Frank Sherman Mitchell
("Kingfish")

Sherman Mitchell thrived on yarn-telling. No one really expected to hear the complete truth when he started to speak; nonetheless, he captivated his audience and held their attention. Some of his fabricated tales could outstretch Pinocchio's nose; but, in a way, they could be described as a loss for words on which to elaborate. He could immediately cause a room to be filled with sounds of roaring laughter. His audience remained entranced as vivid images were created before their eyes. He always expressed sincerity as if he believed what he was telling, even though no one else in the room was fully convinced.

Sherman, like most of the other patrons, was a local farmer and an avid sportsman, especially with his fishing (somewhat fishy) talents. Some men who gathered around the stove jokingly referred to Sherman as the "biggest liar" ever known; however, I prefer to call him one of the "best comedians." Radio and television comedians had nothing on him. He could put them all to shame. His exaggerated truths remain notorious among those who knew him or knew of him. His yarn renderings should have been entered in the "Guinness Book of World Records."

He would "spin a good yarn" and dole out "malarkey" to anyone who dared listen to him. Those who knew him well were not gullible enough to always believe him. Whether you were convinced by what he said, you were most likely entertained and probably left with a chuckle. Sherman should have been a politician because he possessed the innate ability to fabricate information with little or no effort, no matter what the subject.

As was tradition, the fishermen would come to the store and brag about their catch of the day. Some caught the biggest bass, while others caught the biggest catfish or bream. The trusty scales that sat in the back room of the store served to settle the argument, if the fisherman brought along his prized catch. Sherman, somehow, never seemed to bring his biggest catch. Not to be outdone over the big fish catch, he told about the day he took his son, Ned, fishing.

"That boy of mine caught a fish so big that the suction dried up the whole pond when he reined it in!"

On another occasion, Sherman went fishing for a much sought-after catfish in a local pond that had an abandoned car submerged in the water on the bottom of the pond. He recounted the events leading up to his catch.

"I leaned back and cast my line into the pond. That old catfish went right by my fishing line, swam inside that old car and rolled up the window."

These were just two examples of his fishing tales that became immortalized as "the catch of the day" and "the catch that got away."

When the men were discussing their vegetable gardens and the healthy crops they had produced, Sherman could not wait to tell them about his running butterbeans.

"My butterbeans were so healthy and the vines were so tall that they left the field, ran up a light pole, and then travelled some fifteen to twenty miles, ending up in Wake Forest. Why, folks were picking butterbeans from those vines and sending me checks in the mail for weeks to come. They sure were some good folks!"

Sometime later when asked again about his butterbean production, Sherman offered a somewhat modifiable explanation. He did, after all, have the innate ability to provide a variety of explanations about the same subject, depending on just how mischievous he felt at the time he was responding to the question.

"The vines on my butterbeans grew so tall that I let them run up the telephone pole and along the telephone lines all the way to Wale Forest. I got me a stepladder and went to picking them butterbeans. By the time I got to Wake Forest, I had picked thirty-five bushels of butterbeans. I sold them to a store in Wake Forest and brought the money home. I didn't even have to shell them."

Without a doubt, Sherman probably quoted some outrageous amount he had received for the sale of these beans.

Once the vegetables had been picked and shelled, it became time for canning the produce. Sherman bought his wife, Arthelia, a new pressure cooker.

"I stopped by the rock quarry and bought a load of number three stone, brought it home, and cooked it in that new pressure cooker. Within fifteen minutes, that cooker had crushed the rock so fine you could mash it with a fork."

That must have been a powerful pressure cooker. As the saying goes, "they sure don't make equipment like that anymore!"

Jimmy Pearce witnessed one of Sherman's contributions to a conversation held among a group of the local farmers about their tobacco crops. In Sherman's words:

"My stalks of tobacco were so big that the crows built a nest in the tops. When we tried to prime the tobacco, we had to cut the leaves off with a chain saw."

That must have been some tobacco crop. It would have been interesting, to say the least, if he had described his means of curing this tobacco and the method he chose to transport it to the sales warehouse. Undoubtedly, that would be another gigantic tale that did not disappoint his audience.

Sherman died in 1979 at the age of sixty-six. Just before he passed away, one of his friends, Lester Barham, visited with him. Sherman had lost much weight and was very frail. He had just returned home from a visit to his doctor. He told Lester he didn't know if he would be able to follow his doctor's orders.

"That blamed doctor wants me to eat twenty pounds of rice a day."

While Lester envisioned the enormous sight one's body would be because of eating that much rice a day, it took him a moment to realize he, once again, had been "duped" by the humorous antics of Sherman. Lester was amazed, not at the whopper that had so easily been slipped into their conversation; but, that even in his weak and frail condition, the "Kingfish" could still manage to provoke laughter from his listener. His countless tales were truly a remarkable feat and he was an unforgettable man.

Frank Sherman Mitchell ("Kingfish")

(2)
Zollie Thomas Pearce
("The Whittler")

    For Mr. Zollie Pearce carving wooden figurines was a favorite pastime. Long before the introduction of high-speed power tools, with his trusty pocket knife and the patience of Job, he could work miracles with a piece of wood.

    Daddy had a whetstone at the store which was used for sharpening knives. The farmers would use it to sharpen their small farm tools and their pocket knives. Of course, Mr. Zollie would always use the whetstone to sharpen his pocket knife before he sat down and began his whittling. He loved sitting on one of the tobacco warehouse benches under the front shelter of our store with his well-sharpened pocket knife in one hand and a carefully chosen wooden stick in the other. He was a skilled whittler of wood; who, with smooth stroking, gentle pressure, and preciseness of control, could change the image of a plain, and often time ugly, piece of wood into a beautiful exhibition of artwork. Thoroughly engrossed in his endeavor, he never stopped to shake off the pile of wood shavings that covered the pant legs of his overalls and the tops of his shoes. Needless to say, Mr. Zollie never had to purchase broom handles nor hoe and rake handles which Daddy had for sale in the store. All he had to do was grab a long tree branch and whittle away. Walla, instant handle!

    Not only did he whittle for his enjoyment but also for the enjoyment of those of us who admired his creative work. He delighted both kids and adults with the way he could whittle so many different and unique jumping jacks and dancing figurines. He cleverly maneuvered them at the end of a long string and presented his own private puppet show. Often, he would carve farm animals and farm buildings. He gave these carvings to his daughter to be used in her teaching kindergarten and first-grade students in different schools from Virginia to Florida.

    History tells us that the tradition of whittling has been passed down for centuries. However, Mr. Zollie was the only person I ever had first-hand knowledge of who practiced this craft. I could sit for hours and watch him as he masterfully turned a common twig from a tree branch at the side of the store into a shape that exploded with beauty and creative imagination. He would whittle away the bark from a long stick and smooth down the splinters and knots. Next, he would whittle a curve on one end of the stick and a point on the other. To my amazement, he had whittled out a walking cane. I laughed heartedly as he jokingly hobbled about leaning on his trusty cane for support.

A gentle and easy-going man, Mr. Zollie never whittled with the intention of making money from his finished product. In fact, quite often, he would present his creation to one of his admirers who watched him work and then gazed at his precision-detailed piece of art. (Another contribution to "in-store" education). His timeless craftsmanship was spellbinding, the fascination which shall forever remain embedded in my childhood memories of my "store buddies."

Eacho Richards and Zollie Pearce

(3)
John "Eacho" Richards

Mr. Eacho and Mr. Zollie were neighbors and best friends. Their treasured friendship was evident as they sat back on the store benches and exchanged comic-filled stories. They each had fishing ponds on their farms where they welcomed friends to go fishing.

Mr. Eacho possessed a humble personality and a quick wit. Though he had a visible calmness about him, I suspected he could become demanding, if necessary. He was a picture of pride and intellect with a sense of humor that added flavor to his conversations. He could even be described as charismatic.

He did not dress in overalls like those worn by most of the customers. Rather, he usually had a sweater worn over his buttoned-down shirt. Instead of a farm hat, he wore a cap, which was always tilted on his head. He wore thick glasses that made his eyes appear huge when he looked at you. His granddaughter, Lyn Massey, compared the lens of his glasses to the glass bottom of a Coca Cola bottle. This was part of the uniqueness that separated him from the norm around the potbellied stove.

Occasionally, when there was no one in the store but him and Mr. Zollie, he would reach over and turn on the radio that the sports enthusiasts "hogged" when a ballgame was on. Mr. Eacho, however, preferred to listen to music on the radio. A few times I even heard him softly sing along. I loved to hear him sing but never drew attention to the fact that I was around the corner listening.

Not only did he grow tobacco on his farm, but he also had an orchard filled with fruit trees. He made cider from the apples and peaches from his trees and often shared his "juices" with his friends at the store. He was also guilty of once-in-awhile "partaking" of the "recipe" (as it was referred to on "The Waltons" television series.) His granddaughter remembers hearing the story about a time when "his wife locked him in the smokehouse all night for having too much to drink."

Like so many others in the store, he loved his snuff. He would dip that snuff and spit a "wad" into the cheese-box spittoon beside the stove. His aim wasn't always very accurate. Occasionally, he missed the box and the deposit landed on the floor beside it. He had been known to splatter a little on a piece of wood on which Mr. Zollie was whittling away. I always believed he deliberately did that because he would shift his body to the side and place his hand over his smiling mouth.

When Mr. Eacho finished his visit to the store, he stopped by the candy case on his way out. He picked out special pieces of candy, placed them in a little bag, and carried the goodies home to his granddaughter.

Once comfortably settled in his green 1951 Chevrolet truck, he would drive away from the store. The Lord was definitely with him because he never stopped to look in either direction to assure it was safe before he headed for home. To quote Lyn,

"He always thought he was the only one on the road."

Mr. Eacho fell and broke his hip in 1963; after which, he required the use of a cane to assist him walking. He passed away in 1966. Lyn submitted a fitting tribute to her grandfather when she wrote, "On February 2, 1966 a legend left 'The County Line.' "

And, may I add, O.B. Gay's store lost another treasured "legend!"

(4)
Ronald "Lytchford" Gay, Sr.

Lytchford was a prominent farmer in the neighborhood who frequented the store but refrained from participation in the latest gossip. Some of the men urged him to contribute to the conversation. As if to imply he did not hear the question, he stood motionless and pushed his hands farther down in the pockets of his bib-overalls. He smiled and responded with a light-hearted chuckle. Maybe he heard them but did not feel compelled to respond. However, if the subject being discussed pertained to tobacco crops, he paused for a few minutes and exchanged information about the progress of planting, harvesting and marketing. He was passionate about his work in crop rotation and land preservation. His picturesque-landscaped fields spoke volumes about his determination to afford the necessary care and maintenance to assure successful farm-crop production from one year to the next, and beyond.

Lytchford was a man of few words. He was a very alert individual but remained reserved when surrounded by others. He attentively listened to conversations and refused to participate in heated arguments. He quietly listened and observed whether he was occupying a pew in Bethlehem Baptist Church or standing in the middle of O. B. Gay's store.

My cousin, Kim, shared her observations of "Mr. Lytchford" when business meetings were held at church. She compared him with the E.F. Hutton commercials once heard on television. People would stop and listen when E.F. Hutton spoke and the same was true when Lytchford Gay felt compelled to speak out on an issue. A hush fell over the room and a fixation of undivided attention evolved.

The one and only time I ever heard him vocalize loudly was one morning when I exited my house and headed for my car to leave for work. He was driving his tractor from his house to the store. We waved at each other and I turned to get in my car. All at once, there was a horrible sounding thud, followed by crashing metal and a loud yell coming from Lytchford. His neighbor, Ronnie Perry, blinded by the bright morning sunlight, did not see the tractor and ran into the back of it. Consequently, the forceful blow to the rear of the tractor caused it to break in half. As a result, Lytchford was trapped beneath the wreckage.

Ronnie jumped out of his truck and ran to him. Lytchford was on the ground beneath the split sections of the tractor. Ronnie approached him and said,

"I'm so sorry! The sun was shining so bright it blocked my vision. I didn't even know you were on the road until my truck hit you."

Ronnie profusely continued to apologize; but, Lytchford remained in his customary silent state.

Fortunately, there were several men at the store. They arrived on the scene and immediately helped him move away from the tractor.

Normally you would expect someone who had undergone this near-death accident to be exasperated and lash out. Not Lytchford, he was visibly shaken and his face turned bright red, but he quietly shook his head and welcomed the assistance of those gathered around him. Fortunately, he survived the incident without any broken bones; however, at that very moment, he probably suffered a broken spirit.

He returned to the store the next day. His cautious movements made it evident the muscles in his body suffered from pain. However, standing proud in his bib overalls, his flannel shirt and his friendly smile, he was back in control. He just chuckled when the men attempted to tease him about his tractor incident.

Lytchford did not believe in wasting time nor money. He spent his money wisely and welcomed any opportunity to save. He bought drinks and nabs from the store and spent much time on the road travelling back and forth to make those purchases. He approached Daddy and asked if he could begin making his purchases in bulk to conserve expense. Daddy ordered extra boxes of nabs and other snacks from the salesmen, and arranged to have a separate order of drinks to meet the needs of Lytchford. At that time, wholesale distributors delivered products only to retail establishments.

Ronald "Lytchford" Gay, Sr.

After some "string pulling," Daddy convinced the driver to drop off drinks at Lytchford's farm prior to making a regular drop at the store. This was just another example of how friends and neighbors willingly shared with each other and worked together. And subsequently, maybe it was proof positive that a "winning smile (ie, Lytchford's trademark) goes a long way."

(5)
Howard Marshall Phillips
("Teen")

    Teen was not your typical bib-overall wearing, dirt-growing farmer. He neatly dressed in casual clothes and was a light-hearted, no-nonsense individual. He became the blunt of some of the farmers' teasing. The men would accuse him of never leaving home without first being assured that someone was always there to "guard his large trunk full of money." They continued to imply that his relative, referred to as "Punk" Perry, who resided at the same house, had money horded from the sale of moonshine whiskey. Teen never afforded the men satisfaction of confirming their accusations nor denying them. Refusing to be intimidated by their antics, he just shrugged his shoulders and walked away.

    Since O. B. Gay's store was almost on the Wake/Franklin county line, the suggestion of some moonshine activity in the area was not out of the realm of possibility. After all, Franklin County was rumored to be the "Moonshine Capital of the World." Moonshine tales, with their comical orations, were as colorful as the potbellied stove yarn spinners. These tales added to the usual country store blabbering that took place in the cold of winter when the men would "track out" from the busy farming.

    I, however, was more captivated by the five-hundred-dollar bill that Teen carried in his wallet. He loved to remove the bill from his wallet and boast,

"How many of y'all have ever seen one of these?"

"I was in 'Lerisberg' (Louisburg) at the bank when the truck brought the money in. This here is one of the first five hundred bills ever printed."

With a smirk, and probably seizing the opportunity to get back at them for their teasing, he continued,

"I doubt any of y'all will ever own one of these bills."

He marveled in delight at the expressions on their faces. Ah, sweet payback!

    The men may not have been impressed, but this budding numismatist looked forward to seeing him reach into his wallet and remove another fresh from the bank currency issue. At that time, my collection consisted of Indian head pennies Daddy saved out for me. Some of them were covered with sticky tobacco gum or dirty snuff and the dates on them were invisible even with a Sherlock Holmes magnifying glass. Nothing a little soap and water couldn't improve. I vowed to one day become an owner of one of those five hundred dollar bills and add it to my collection. Regretfully, before I could accomplish the feat, the Federal Reserve System, on July 14, 1969, discontinued printing this high-denominational currency. Only a few of those bills remained in existence and they quickly became collectors' items with an accompanying "ridiculous" purchase price. That prospect was definitely out of my league!

Teen remained one of my favorite store customers. It deeply saddened me when years later he and Daddy had a "falling out" over a tobacco land rental agreement and he chose to no longer patronize our store. Regretfully, money remained an underlying culprit.

Howard "Teen" Phillips

(6)
Agerford Oliver Gay
("A. O.")

In the late 1940s, Daddy's brother A.O. Gay was enjoying the single life. He lived with his mama on a small farm in Franklin County. Lathering himself in Old Spice aftershave lotion, he entered the store "smelling good." He always managed to hang around the front area of the store whenever he spotted a pretty young lady approaching the door. I loved to watch him turn on the charm, especially when a certain Baker girl came in the store.

One cold afternoon in December, A.O. and his girlfriend, Ethelene, came in the store holding a bag of small balloons. He held up the bag and asked Daddy,

"Have you got any balls of tobacco thread left over from the summer?"

Daddy handed him two balls of thread. He wondered what his mischievous brother was up to now. He watched as the two strolled back to A.O.'s bright red 1949 Mercury convertible where A.O.'s best friend, Ebbie Martin, Jr., and his wife Alice, were waiting for them.

A.O. turned around and said,

"Oh yeah, I need to fill my car up with gas. Put that on the books. I will pay you next week."

Then "show off"" A.O. left a couple of tail spins as they drove away.

When he returned to the store the following week, he couldn't wait to tell the other men about the exciting night the four of them had after they left the store.

"We rode down to Wilson and had a little fun spreading good cheer on the streets. Me and Ebbie blew up a bunch of them balloons. The girls cut some of the tobacco-thread off and made long strings to tie to the balloons. We were planning to roll the windows down and ride around with the balloons hanging out the door. After downing a few drinks, somehow that didn't seem like too much fun. So we decided to put the top back on my convertible. Hell, we were feeling so good it didn't matter that it was freezing weather outside. We were having a blast." Once the customers displayed their amusement, A.O. continued,

"We rode up and down the streets in Wilson. We waved balloons and wished everybody a 'Merry Christmas.' That's when we noticed a car one street over slowing down. The car was going in the opposite direction from us; but, we managed to catch a glimpse of red lights attached to its roof. That was the end of our fun. We made a fast exit out of that town and didn't look back. Once safely out of the city limits, we pulled over and put the top back up on the car. We laughed all the way back home."

A.O. was a fun-loving individual. He loved his Ford trucks. Every time he bought a new truck, it always had to be a Ford purchased straight from the factory with a special-made door. The door on the driver's side had a hollowed-out space hidden behind the panel. There he would place his bottle of homemade scuppernong grape wine and carefully replace the panel as a disguise for any officer that might go through his vehicle in search of alcoholic beverages. Sometimes, his latest purchase of whiskey from the ABC store occupied that hidden space.

A.O. Gay

(7)
Lewis Evans Lloyd
("Jack")

    Lewis "Jack" Lloyd was by trade a mechanic who worked on the bread making machines at Continental Baking Company or what we recognized as "Wonder Bread." His dad, Lonnie Lloyd, was the proprietor who ran the country store before Daddy purchased it. Understandably, Jack had good memories of time spent at his own dad's store and welcomed the opportunity, when away from his job in Raleigh, to relax in that same atmosphere. He worked the night shift which allowed him time during the day to converse with the local patrons.
    Though Jack enjoyed talking with the men at the store, he was a man that wanted to be busy working. Hence, whenever the opportunity availed, he offered his services as an interior house painter. He was a very meticulous painter. Many hours I watched as he applied paint to the walls of our home without spilling a drop on the floors or the window panes. He amazed me with his precision and overall beauty of the end project. With a steady hand, he methodically applied the paint-filled brush to the walls in a rhythmic manner. He never missed a stroke even when I insidiously requested weird color combinations for my bedroom and our living room. When he finished, he turned and smiled,
    "See, I told you I could do it. The colors you picked weren't quite as bad as I thought they would be when I first mixed the paint," he said with a laugh.
    History, a subject I totally loathed in high school, began to pleasantly unfold before me as I listened to Jack talk about his military experiences and the places he traveled. He served his country during World War II as a Steward's Mate First Class with the U.S. Merchant Marines. One of his duties was to cook meals that were not only wholesome but left the seamen with a full belly and a smile on their face. True to his character, Jack worked diligently in his cooking duties and developed many culinary skills.
    Jack shared many events about his military career and his fellow seamen. His many stories, both good and bad, added flavor to topics discussed around the potbellied stove.

Jack Lloyd

Additionally, Jack enlightened younger patrons on what to expect from employers, in the business world, once a person neared retirement age. His revelations gave insight and eye-opening realization of the cruelty of the "real world." He described how industrial factories created heavy workloads and a workplace environment that often proved detrimental to the health and wellbeing of senior employees. He emphasized that stress derived from this situation often caused the victim to suffer a stroke or heart attack, sometimes resulting in permanent disability or even death.

Jack was one of the last patrons to visit with my parents at their store. Daddy gave him the original door knobs from the old store that Mr. Lonnie Lloyd ran. Sadly, Jack passed away about three weeks after we closed the store. The stroke he suffered from work-related stress prevented him from realizing his long-awaited dream of retiring with time to enjoy the "golden years" of his life.

(8)

James Ruffin Whitley
(Mr. Jim)

Among the men of this area, the use of nicknames was commonplace when they referred to a spouse, a sibling, a child or grandchild, a neighbor, or a friend. Mr. Jim extended this practice one step further. He referred to his Allis Chambers tractor as "Alice," not only giving it a name, but a gender as well.

He never had a driver's license. When asked why he did not have a license to drive, he replied,

"I don't need a license as long as I have my two feet and my tractor."

Before he bought his tractor, he always walked to the store. The bottom of his feet must have been tough as leather because he walked miles along the unpaved road. I never saw him with shoes on, not even in the cold weather. He loved that "barefoot feeling," a downhome Carolinian through and through; and to the best of my knowledge, he never even drank a "mountain dew."

His trusted white dog, Trixie, often rode with him on the tractor when he drove to the store. Trixie always waited patiently and never jumped down from the tractor while Mr. Jim went inside.

Mr. Jim spoke with the other patrons; however, he chose not to engage in the busy talk around the stove. He was a friendly man, with a free-willed-wit, who never met a stranger. He never spoke negatively against another person. He conversed briefly while he made his purchases and asked daddy to assist him at the pump outside. Once he filled the tractor's gas tank, he and Trixie headed home.

Like so many other men who patronized daddy's store, Mr. Jim loved to fish. His satisfaction of this relaxing sport lay not in the local ponds catching brim and bass. Rather, he loved to fish on the river and returned home with his prize catches of the day, the hefty catfish.

He loved chit lings and stocked-up on them annually at hog-killing time. I sure was glad he never used them as part of the barter system at the store. He once offered to share some of those awful things (Ugh!) with me; but, I respectfully declined his generosity.

Mr. Jim and his wife had eight children. He taught them, at a very early age, to be responsible and productive. He planted an acre of cucumbers and assigned each child their very own row and made them responsible for gathering the produce from the vines. He stressed the length and size to be picked and discouraged waste. He was adamant that daily care be taken to assure satisfactory yield. Cucumbers had to be picked at a precise time. None could grow too big for harvesting or they would become useless when time came for processing. There was no "passing the buck" allowed. He expected each child to be responsible for their assigned row only; and, if they fell short of his expectations, there were consequences.

He was a creature of habit with a way of stretching a dollar. Even to the day of his death, once a month when he received his check in the mail, his daughter drove him to the grocery store where he purchased the same four staples for his household. He bought sugar, flour, tea and coffee always in large bags to assure there was enough to last throughout the entire month. This practice was conceivably carried forward from the Great Depression Era of the 1930's.

He loved his "white lightening" and sometimes drank it out of a fruit jar. He never bothered anyone when he drank. He always remained in his bedroom or some area away from everyone else. The only day he drank his brew was on Saturday. That allowed him time to sleep it off on Sunday and still be ready for the new work week on Monday morning.

Mr. Jim was completely toothless; but, that never hindered him from eating what he desired, whether it was an apple, corn on the cob, meat or anything else that normally required a strong set of teeth. It certainly never prevented him from smoking his hand-rolled cigarettes.

He preferred to roll his own cigarettes as opposed to purchasing the brand name, which had been packaged at a factory. Instead of cigarettes by the pack, he bought a pouch filled with loose tobacco pieces and tied at the top by a string. His brand of choice was Old Advertiser Smoking Tobacco. When he visited the store he always asked for his favorite brand and for a book of OCB Cigarette Rolling Papers. He preferred this brand because the papers were not gummed and did not leave an unpleasant taste in his mouth when he sealed them.

The speed with which he rolled his cigarette could be described as "faster than a speeding bullet" (from the superman commercials). He displayed that "hand is quicker than the eye" magic. In addition, he possessed uncanny coordination when he removed one of the soft, white rolling papers from its book and held it in one hand between his thumb and his middle finger. With his other hand he, in a rhythmic manner, evenly spread a small amount of the tobacco in a thin line along the surface of the paper. He took the paper in both hands and used his thumbs to roll the cigarette. Once the paper was tight around the tobacco, he held the edge up to his tongue. Then, he applied a steady stream of saliva to the paper and pressed it until it smoothly sealed.

His cigarettes were always very thin and properly packed with few, if any, spills of tobacco in the process. Because of the speed and precision with which he rolled them, I found it impossible to determine if he, like the other men, twisted either end of the cigarette. I assume he never pinched off any tobacco hanging from the ends because there was no tobacco residue left behind. He would have been an ideal choice for a television commercial for R.J. Reynolds Tobacco Co. He was as methodical as a well-oiled, mass production, cigarette assembly machine.

His daughter shared with me a time when Mr. Jim accompanied his family to the beach and spent some time out on the pier. It was there he removed his tobacco pouch from his bib pocket and rolled a cigarette. Local authorities watched as he placed the cigarette to his lips. They approached him and accused him of smoking marijuana. Just before the officers placed him under arrest, his son walked up. He explained that his dad was not smoking anything but good old American tobacco, not an illegal substance; and, that he had always rolled his own cigarettes. No charges were filed and no arrest was made.

Mr. Jim Whitley, another one-of-a-kind man who left an impression!

Mr. and Mrs. Jim Whitley

(9)

Irey Leonard Gay
(The "Country Store Lawyer"}

Leonard was a farmer, never a lawyer; and, he never had the opportunity to watch the television series about a country lawyer which premiered twenty-three years after his death. Yet, he could best be described as the fictional Georgia criminal defense attorney, Ben Matlock, portrayed by North Carolina's own Andy Griffith.

Griffith in his role as Matlock displayed, before a courtroom filled with people, the same facial expressions and mannerisms that were so characteristic of Leonard's command of the floor when he addressed the store patrons.

Speaking in his slow Southern drawl, Leonard stood before the men in the store and required unyielding attention when he talked. Dressed in a long-sleeved shirt, "bib" overalls and big hat, his attire bared little resemblance to the loose-fitted suit worn by Matlock.

When Leonard spoke, his head tilted and his hands extended in several different directions as if to emphasize a point he was attempting to make. He didn't speak with his mouth freely opened. With a subdued smile, his bottom lip slightly extended when he talked. In a heated conversation, his lips tended to tighten and turn down at the ends.

Not unlike Matlock, his subtle gestures could, at times, be deemed cantankerous. An air of confidence was evident by his gruff and gregarious tone. When he felt confident he had delivered a speech that captured their attention, he, like the Matlock character, would slightly tilt his head to the side and reveal a "smirk" of satisfaction.

If Leonard did not receive the attention he commanded, he became impatient and his forehead furrowed,

"You boys listen up! I've got something to say."

Leonard was openly vocal with his expressions. However, in response to the expressions of others, he oftentimes simply grunted,

"Humph."

After delivering his "spill," he often encouraged his son, Aubrey, to take center stage. Leonard did not hesitate to demand undivided attention for his son.

Leonard's idiosyncrasies and his subtleness were not always welcomed by everyone. He left an impressionable mark on the history of the old country store, a tradition his son proudly continued.

In conjunction with the Griffith and Gay comparisons already addressed in the foregoing statements, the following footnote adds yet another "interesting" similarity.

Both Leonard Gay and Andy Griffith died in their North Carolina homes because of a heart attack.

Ruth, Aubrey, & Leonard Gay

(10)
Aubrey Leonard Gay
(The World Traveler)

Like so many others of his generation, Aubrey vowed not to follow in the footsteps of his father and other men in the community and choose farming as his occupation. To that end, he attended and graduated from Louisburg College and N.C. State University. For a short while, he worked with a major chemical company as a fertilizer salesman. Eventually he accepted a position as the agricultural teacher at Franklinton High School. This position allowed him summer months off to travel abroad.

Like his dad Leonard, Aubrey had a "gift of gab" and what better place to exercise that gift than before a captivated audience at the old country store. He would polish-off his peanut-laced bottle of R.C. Cola, wipe his mouth, and set the stage for an evening of "one-sided' conversation. Aubrey, in a sense, was a "carbon copy" of his dad. He, too, fell into the genre of the Griffith persona.

Both father and son could audibly be identified upon entering a country store. Leonard's famous "you boys" became the attention-getter used by his son. Speeches rendered by Aubrey possessed more flair. He had more topics to discuss than farming, hunting and fishing; subjects which he personally had very little interest. He was a world traveler and welcomed every opportunity to talk about his trips abroad. He was never at a loss for words!

One night, the men were discussing crime in America and how convicted felons were released from prison and returned to society only to repeat the same crime again. Aubrey quickly shared with them the crime prevention methods he learned about while visiting countries in the Middle East.

"Those officials had no tolerance for crime. For instance, a man caught stealing was punished by having his hand cut off for the first offense. If there failed to be a mending of his ways and he was caught again for the same offense, he was beheaded. Problem solved!"

He told of how he and his wife, Marie, visited stores and there were no bars on the windows. Merchants had no fear of robbery.

They visited a jewelry store in a shopping center.

"The jewelry was laid out in the open. None of the pieces were concealed, not even those expensive pieces laced with gold. Honesty was the norm."

I enjoyed listening to him tell about his travels. It fell right in with my "in-store-education." It was a geography lesson that made you feel like you had visited the place he talked about.

His enthusiasm never wavered when he had the attention of someone with whom to share his travel experiences. He and his wife travelled around the world three times, made two safari trips to Africa and one safari trip to Asia. They boarded a cruise ship and visited Antarctica. In addition to these trips, they visited 113 different countries. Before each trip, he started planning every place he wanted to visit and how many historical sights, landmarks, etc. could be included in that trip. Often, he would begin planning the next trip almost as soon as he returned home from his last trip; sometimes a year in advance.

Aubrey and Marie Gay 2001 Anger Wat, Cambodia

Aubrey and Marie Gay 2003 Chile Research Station Antarctica

He received a little more response from the store customers when he told of his travels in the United States. Some of the other men were familiar with the places he described and others had family members outside North Carolina. Subsequently, their interest peeked and he once again commanded their undivided attention. He had visited all fifty states and all the provinces in Canada.

His last trip was again abroad. This time it was to Venezuela. He and Marie went to see Angel Falls, the tallest falls in the world.

After he returned home from this trip, he started losing weight and had no interest in planning another trip.

Additionally, his trips to the local stores became fewer and far between. His zest for life, the contributing factor for holding his audience captive, slowly began to dwindle. He had very little to say to anyone.

This highly-motivated, vocally-strong, floor-demanding, Matlock/Griffith charismatic speaker had grown silent and removed himself from the country-store podium. But, his legacy will forever reign.

He was stricken with Guillain-Barre Syndrome in 2010 and did not recover from this disablement. This syndrome was a major contributing factor to his death on May 3rd of that same year.

Another footnote, Griffith was stricken with the same rare Guillain-Barre Syndrome in 1983 and was unable to walk for a period of seven months. Unlike Aubrey, Griffith recovered from this disablement after rehabilitation.

(11)
Clarence Edward Duke, Sr.
(The Wave)

Mr. Clarence resided near the stores at Hopkins Cross Roads, but he often frequented Daddy's store. I remember him as a gentle man with a pleasing personality and an open friendliness. His "words of wisdom" resonated with me throughout my childhood and especially when I reached senior citizen status.

I envisioned him as the most popular man in the whole community because he seemed to know everybody. No matter if the driver was in his familiar vehicle or had just purchased a new model, Mr. Clarence still seemed to know who was behind the wheel. He would immediately throw his hand up and wave at the passerby. They, in turn, would wave back at him. He must have liked everyone.

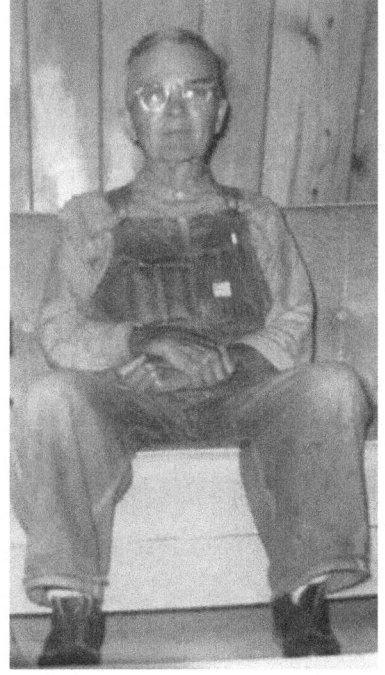

Clarence Duke

One day I was sitting on the bench located under the store shelter when Mr. Clarence drove up. He got out of his car and stopped by the bench to greet me. I looked up at him and asked,

"Mr. Clarence, why do you wave at every car that goes by?"

He politely replied,

"Someday you will understand. At my age, I can't see well enough to recognize who is driving a car or truck down the road. So, I wave at everybody. That way, I won't insult anyone. Nobody can call me 'stuck up' because I didn't wave at them."

Dear Mr. Clarence, at my age now, I understand what you meant! Don't forget to WAVE.

(12)

Eddie "The Healer" Blackley
(The Healer)

Some store patrons said Mr. Eddie was the only farmer around who could borrow ninety-five dollars at the beginning of a farm year and feed a family of eleven the entire year on that amount. He was sometimes labeled the "cleverest" farmer around. Obviously, like other farm owners of that period, most of the food was from their own garden and meat from the farm animals.

His love for animals and his insightful way of caring for them gained him the reputation of being a self-made veterinarian. He may not have been authorized to treat diseases and injuries of the animals; but, in the opinion of those in the community, he was qualified. Farmers from far and wide would call on him to "doctor" their horses, mules, goats and all their other animals when they required medical attention.

To me Mr. Eddie was the "Great Healer." As a child, I suffered from asthma. Trips to doctors in search of a cure proved fruitless. Mother had almost given up on a cure until Mr. Eddie approached her and asked if he could administer his special cure for asthma. She consented and he returned a few days later and asked me to accompany him to the front porch of our house. He told Mother no one could come but me.

Mr. Eddie explained to me that he had "magical powers." I became a little scared because I had heard that he loved goats and I was silently praying,

"Lord, please don't let me have to drink goat's milk! I think I'm going to barf."

Anyway, we sat down on the steps of our front porch and he began talking to me.

"There is nothing to be afraid of. You can trust me. I'm going to tell you how to get rid of that ole asthma. Do you want me to help you?"

I nodded my head and he then cautioned me,

"There is only one condition. You cannot tell anyone what my secret is. If you tell anyone about my magical powers they will not work and your asthma will get worse."

I agreed to his terms. He placed a small cloth bag on the porch floor beside him. Then he told me to go into the house and find one of my favorite hair bows and bring it to him. I was so scared to tell anyone what words he uttered and what powers he put on me that, to this day, I still can't remember how he rid me of the asthma.

The only thing I can recall is, after he finished with his mumble-jumble words, he told me to stand with my back to the porch wall beside the door frame. He removed a pencil from his pocket and made a straight mark on the wall directly above my head. Then he made another mark a couple of spaces above the long mark and wrote a "fat" X on the second mark.

He told me,

"When the top of your head becomes level with the bottom of the big X, your asthma will be gone."

It worked! My own "country doctor" remained another of my favorite people.

Eddie "The Healer" Blackley

(13)
Hilary James Pearce
("Possum")

Mr. "Possum" Pearce was a daily patron to the store and someone I dearly loved to talk to because of his great sense of humor. He had a house full of boys and we all rode on the same school bus. I was attracted to one of them in particular. Mother was very strict about girlfriend/boyfriend relationships and I didn't dare let her know I was "sweet" on a boy in the neighborhood. In fact, I wouldn't admit it to anyone, not even the Pearce boy.

One day Mr. Possum came into the store and I was walking around with a bad case of hiccups. I had tried every suggestion that people gave me to stop the hiccups but nothing seemed to work. Suddenly, Mr. Possum turned to Daddy and said,

"Oris I need to tell you something about your daughter and my son."

I gasped,

"What on earth was he talking about?"

I knew well that I had told no one how I felt about his son. I wondered who in the world gave him that information. I stopped dead in my tracks.

My fear of what he was going to reveal to my daddy about his son was magnified to the extent I completely forgot about those hiccups.

Mr. Possum started laughing as my face burned with embarrassment,

"Girl, don't get so mad. Nobody said anything to me about you and my boy. I was just trying to scare you enough to make you stop hiccupping. I think it worked?!"

My fear and anger at him for his "threat" remained with me for quite some time to come. He tried over and over to apologize to me. Not only was I upset over what he said, I no longer felt

"Possum" Pearce

confident in his presence, a heartbreaking feeling for me because I always was eager to talk with him.

Time passed and this incidence became a great source of laughter between me and Mr. Possum. Who could not like this man who had a comical sense of humor and wit that made even the sternest person unable to suppress a smile.

Despite the fact he gave me the scare of my life, my memory of time spent around him at the country store was a fun experience. He especially added character and humor when he joined in the conversations swapped around the old potbellied stove.

Chapter Eighteen

FAMILIAR SURNAMES AND NICKNAMES

During the fifty-year span of O.B. Gay's store, from 1933 to 1983, most people in the area were either related to or married to someone who was related to another individual in the community. Surnames were simple and family members were easily identifiable by their last name. The last names of most of the customers at Daddy's store were as follows:

Arnold	Baker	Barham	Belvin	Blackley	Bunn
Carter	Denton				
Duke	Ferrell	Fowler	Gay	Hopkins	Horton
Jackson	Johnson				
King	Lloyd	Martin	Mitchell	Mullins	Murray
Pearce	Perry				
Phillips	Privette	Pulley	Richards	Rogers	Upchurch
Whitley	Wright				

"Doc" Baker

The only name during that period that sounded strange around the "County Line" was Liborio and he was married to a Perry, so he was accepted.

Adrian and Lettie Murray

Now in 2016, there is a tremendous array of surnames who patronize the community's latest (2013) convenience store, County Line Grocery & Grill, owned and operated by father and son, Henry and David Bunn. Some of today's surnames are hard, if not impossible, to pronounce. Seldom will you find a group of people in the store that share the same last name. People are usually referred to by their first name only.

Contrastingly, in the 1933 – 1983 fifty-year span, first names were replaced by nicknames, which were prevalent when Daddy's country store business remained in full operation. Even the small store located on this rural property when Daddy first purchased the land was tagged with the nickname "Red Bird."

When strangers came to the store and inquired about someone by their given name, patrons would inquisitively glance at each other as if to say,

"Who the heck are they talking about?"

Often nicknames added substance to the verbalization of a heated argument whether used by children or adults. Some names were traditional, others unique, and many were a result of childhood teasing. Below is a listing of a few of

Grover and Kate Pulley

the nicknames of customers who frequented Daddy's store over the years.

"Dub"	"Pete"	"Peddler"	"Kingfish"
"Monkey"			
"Doc"	"Toad"	"Possum"	"Hoover"
"Biggie"			
"Pie"	"Wink"	"Junior"	"Bubba"
"Chicken"			
"Bud"	"Skeet"	"Sonny"	"Coon"
"Sugar Boy"			
"Sun"	"Smug"	"Butch"	
"Doodle"	"Booger"		
"Red"	"Fella"	"Teen"	"Crip"
"Tweet"			
"Nig"	"Mutt"	"Jack"	"Dink"
"Bird"			
"Boy"	"Goat"	"Shorty"	"Pee Dab"
"Boweavel"			
"Rob"	"Jabo"	"Punk"	"Bittie"
"Buddy"			

Nicknames were as traditional as country stores and carried with them just as many amusingly-eccentric tales.

Some kids in the area loved to telephone a store and ask,
"Is Red there?"
The person who answered the phone usually replied,
"Red who?"
The kids responded,
"Red Pepper! Ain't that hot?"
Then they would laugh when the recipient of the call started fussing and calling them names.

As indicated in the list of nicknames above, one customer at Daddy's store went by the name of "Red." So, when the kids phoned his store and asked for "Red," they received a surprising answer,
"Red, come back here. You've got a telephone call."
Red picked up the phone and said,
"Hello. Hello, is anybody there?"

There was no laughing on the other end of the phone this time. Instead, there was a hushed silence and a speedy click of the phone receiver.

For once, a nickname held an advantage. The men in the store had the last laugh!

Chapter Nineteen

NO NEED FOR COMPETITION

There was no shortage of country stores around for the men to gather. Daddy's store was closed on Sundays and that gave him the opportunity to not be the proprietor but the customer at another store. His favorite gathering place was Pettigrew Gay's store on Gay Road. He left me and Mother at Grandma Gay's for a Sunday visit while he went to sit back and be one of the regulars at Pettigrew's store. Apparently, he could not get enough of the store business six days a week. He spent his one night off visiting another store. While there, he had the chance to talk not only with his brothers but many of his cousins, as well. Almost everyone on that road was related and Sundays nights were like a family reunion for the men folks.

O.B. Gay's store was centrally located in an area where within a three-mile radius there were country stores on almost every corner. Daddy's store rested immediately behind the point where Halifax Road, Youngsville and Hopkins Chapel Road, Zebulon joined. On the Franklin County section (merging onto Old Halifax Road, Pilot-Riley Road and Bethlehem Church Road) of this particular area, there were businesses owned and/or operated by Bob Mullins, Mark Fowler, Worth Perry, James Perry, Clem Pearce, Bruitt Bunn, Junie Upchurch, H.C. Rogers, C.E. Richards and Darius Pearce. On the Wake County section (Hopkins Chapel Road and Fowler Road), there were businesses owned and operated by Ivan Hopkins, Cecil Hopkins, Jessie Bunn, Paul Horton, Billy Hopkins and Sidney Harris. On the opposite Wake County section (Halifax Road, Mitchell Store Road and Zebulon Road), there were businesses owned/operated by Byrd Perry, Billy Mitchell, Mack Perry and Austin Perry.

Luther "Byrd" & Rosa Perry

Competition among these stores was never a real issue. Like those men who patronized the stores, each store issued an inviting welcome to all who entered. Daddy's store had the distinction of resting on what was once the "County Line Ball Club" where the Riley Crossroads team hosted countless baseball games. Other stores in the area offered at least one product or service that was equally unique for their establishment. Following are a few of the specialized differences associated with these stores. Cordell Richards provided many of these facts based on his growing up surrounded by his dad's country store and information he gained, first hand, from other store owners in the community. Additional contributions are from a few other of us "old timers" and our childhood memories.

Mark Fowler's store carried with it the reputation of some people being killed or even hung by the neck on the premises. Whether fact or fiction, those execution stories were repeated by community residents for decades. Many patrons who visited Mr. Mark's store remembered seeing a pair of boxing gloves hanging on the wall. Legend has it that if Mr. Mark sensed one or two of the men wanted to fight, he insisted they go outside. Once outside, someone would draw a big circle in the dirt. Mr. Mark removed the boxing gloves from the store wall, told the "fighters" to put them on and "have at it!" Anxiously anticipating the outcome, other customers gathered around the circled ring. Some even placed a small "wager" on their favored winner.

Another service offered by Mr. Mark at his store was "tying the knot." He was a Justice of the Peace for Franklin County and he performed many marriage ceremonies in this country store setting.

C.E. "Charlie" Richards introduced in his store one treat as its specialty that has, henceforth, never been duplicated or

Millard "Chicken" Murray in front of Austin Perry store

equaled. That delicious treat was his thirst-quenching "pineapple sherbet." Like some others in the community, he had a big wooden ice chest in which huge blocks of ice were placed. With an ice scrapper in his hand, Mr. Charlie put into motion what would become one of the appealing trademarks of his store. Mrs. Rella, his wife, filled a gallon jar with sugar and water. One of them would scrape shavings off the huge block of ice and place it in paper cups or cones. Then they would open a fresh can of crushed pineapple and place some over the crushed ice. Finally, they would pour some of the sugar water over the entire cone or cup and serve. This was a welcome treat for all ages: men, women and children. No one could resist their delicious pineapple sherbet; especially on a sweltering hot summer afternoon, and usually after the evening meal.

Clem Pearce, in his senior years, reached a point in his health where he was almost deaf. Communication with him was awkward because everything had to be repeated in an almost screaming tone for him to hear what you were saying. Some customers hesitated to patronize his store for this reason. This inconvenience never prevented him from always having fresh fish for sale at the end of each week. His customers would be standing at the door of his store and, for once, they never seemed to mind the fact they had to yell at him.

Bruett Bunn ran a store and a repair shop in the same building which was located across from Clem's store, and remained in operation from the mid 1960's to the mid 1970's. His store/shop was where the locals went when they wished to have their vehicles inspected. Years later, he closed his store and pursued an entirely different career. He, along with his son, invested time and effort in a house-moving service which proved to be a very lucrative and rewarding business.

Billy Mitchell's store was in Wake County just prior to the Franklin County line on Mitchell Store Road. The main thing that separated his business from others in the area was the fact he owned, and provided for the pleasure of his customers, the first and only television set in any of the area stores. Every Friday night, men in the community would gather around the television set to watch the Friday Night boxing event. They had to arrive before the boxing match began so they could purchase their soda and snacks for the event. If they arrived too late, they were not permitted to purchase anything because Mr. Billy turned out the store lights when the fight came on and all eyes were "glued" to the television set.

Sidney Harris operated a store located at the end of Fowler Road where it intersected with Zebulon Road. The Perry family actually owned the store. This elongated, wood-framed building was divided into three separate sections. The front section was the general store. The mid-section was a garage where several of the men in the community remember,

"Sidney never worked on a car without using a crowbar."

Finally, the back section was used as Sidney's residence where you could, at times during the middle of the day, find him stretched out and fast asleep on his cot.

Mack Perry closed the small store on the old section of Mitchell Mill Road which had for years been run by his parents, Bud and Oma Perry. After their death, Mack built a new store a few hundred feet upward from the original store and now located on Zebulon Road. (This is the only store, among the ones featured in these articles, that remains in operation as of this year 2017 writing. Known as Mitchell's Store it belongs to Crettie Morgan, widow of Jerry Mitchell, Sr. the former proprietor.) There were probably many unique qualities about this store of which I am unaware. The one thing I associate with Mr. Mack's store: this was the location where all citizens in the precinct went to cast their votes for the political candidate of their choice at election time.

Austin Perry owned and operated a brick-built store on Zebulon Road immediately past where the now Mitchell Mill Road ends at Zebulon Road. His business was in operation from 1941 to 1971. Not only did he avail customers the commodities needed for everyday living; he also opened a grill in his store. Farmers and their work crew rushed in at lunch time to purchase a fresh-grilled meal. Austin's daughters Judi and Janice operated "The Two of Us Beauty Nook" in the rear of his store.

H.C. Rogers ran a store across from Junie Upchurch's store on Old Halifax Road in Franklin County. Under his proprietorship, the focus was removed from general merchandise purchases and centered on providing entertainment for the customers.

A brightly-painted green door welcomed those who chose this location for their "hangout." The business was appropriately called "The Green Door." This store name was the same as when it was previously strictly a general store. With the introduction of a song title by this name and the rumored talk about the new business operations, people were convinced a lot went on behind that door in the late 1950's. This definitely wasn't a place parents allowed their teenagers to visit.

In 1956, Jim Lowe recorded a song entitled "Green Door" in which this question was asked,

"Green Door, what's that secret you're keeping?"

Locals who did not patronize this business began also to ask that same question, especially when the song resounded throughout the building and could audibly be heard when they passed the building while driving down the road.

It was rumored (and confirmed by a gentleman who patronized the store) that the walls were filled with loud music, roaring laughter, heated arguments, alcohol consumption and colorful women. Only the rough and rowdy could be found behind the Green Door.

Recently, another man pointed out to me that Green Door was the eastern version of the wild-west saloons with the poker playing and cheat accusations which ended in gun duels. One big difference, the guns behind the Green Door were not 45 caliber six-shooters. Rather, when two angry men faced off they were peering down the barrel of a shotgun! Ouch! That was NOT your average country-store setting.

As time passed, some of the older store owners rented their business out to new people with new ideas. The number of customers daily patronizing Daddy's store diminished as the new merchants offered prices that threatened to force him out of business. However, this practice never seemed to faze him. He was steadfast and determined to remain proprietor of his country store until he reached his goal of fifty years of service to his community.

I once asked why the under-minding tactics of others didn't bother him. He replied,

"Some of them have undercut my prices. One or two have even boasted that they were going to run me out of business by luring my steady customers away."

He leaned back on the seat in front of the open, side-window. He propped his foot up on the board beneath the shelves, and continued,

"I've watched as their businesses grew real fast; and, then I watched as it slowly began to decline. I've stayed right here and not given in to competitive pressure. I'm still here to welcome my customers back, one by one, when the newness rubs off and they return to the familiar. I don't believe in price wars. Never have, never will! Sooner or later, everything will get back to normal."

Failure was not an option for Daddy. He gained the admiration and loyalty of his long-time patrons and the next generations of patrons that followed them over the years. Those who once came with their parents, matured and continued to patronize his store. Some of the "old timers" even allowed their grandchildren to "tag along" and get a taste of the country store experience.

The traditional country stores persevered, weathered the storms, and withstood all the hardships and inconveniences hurled at them.

Chapter Twenty

SOMETHING MUST BE BREWING

A few times there were many trucks and cars parked outside the store; but, upon entering the store it became evident the drivers of those vehicles were meeting somewhere other than around that old potbellied stove.

Maybe there was a little more competition elsewhere? Where could it be and why would they park their vehicles at one store and go to another?

A few months earlier, some of my store buddies and I took an inquisitive trip through the woods across from Daddy's store. We discovered a "whiskey still" where a fresh batch of "moonshine" was brewing. Christmas season was fast approaching and batches of "white lightning" were being prepared for sale. Of course, they had to make sure they were providing the best brew around. To do that, they willingly took a little "nip" before sealing the bottles.

Meanwhile, we became giggly over our discovery. However, we were afraid the moonshiners would discover we were watching them. Even worse, what if we were caught by the "revenuers?"

One of the boys wanted to wait until the men left and then sample a taste of the brew. The rest of us said,

"No way!"

We would never be able to disguise that smell and we would be in deep trouble when we got home.

Another time, we were at the store and we began to laugh because we were pretty sure that we knew where the missing drivers of those parked vehicles were. We decided to check it out.

Once again, we headed through the woods. We passed the area where we had discovered the "still" and noticed a wood-framed house in the not-too-far distance. As we approached the house, we saw the windows were covered with shutters. No one had lived in that old house for years; yet, we were almost certain there was a light coming from the inside. Sounds of arguing voices resounded from behind those walls. We slowly moved a little closer, careful not to put any pressure on the cracked-wood porch floor. We reached the back door and took turns peering through a small opening beside the door handle.

We looked at each other in dismay. There inside was an old wooden table that looked like it was hand-carved from the sawed-off trunk of one of the huge oak trees that had fallen in the woods alongside the house. Several nail-keg stools surrounded the large table. Smoke filled the room as the men puffed away on their cigarettes. Even through the smoke, we could still see stacks of poker chips and piles of dollar bills on the table. All the nail-keg stools were occupied by men who normally gathered around that old potbellied stove at O.B. Gay's store. The men were not concerned about being hassled by the law because their hideaway was just beyond the county line. In those days, law enforcement officials were not allowed to make an arrest outside their county jurisdiction. Whether they were approached by a Wake County lawman or a Franklin County lawman, they only had to run a few feet to be across the line and untouchable.

Mystery solved. Pieces of the puzzle comfortably fitted together. We fled the scene without incident. Once we reached the end of the path and exited the wooded area, we felt relieved and burst out laughing. We made a promise to each other that this would be our secret forever. (Sorry guys, the "cat is out of the bag.")

Over time, the "stills" were destroyed and The Green Door went out-of-business. Years later, Bob Mullins rented his store to the son of a well-known car dealer in Raleigh, and he turned that establishment into a more civilized tavern. However, the existence of that business was short lived.

The traditional country stores persevered, weathered the storms, and withstood all hurdles of competition thrown at them.

Though the ready availability of alcoholic beverages added flair to some of the other businesses in the area, the choice not to sell alcohol remained the defining constant at O.B. Gay's store.

Chapter Twenty-One

BEER & WINE SALES CONFLICT

O. B. Gay's store survived the post-depression era but years later fell victim to declining sales. During the 1970s, it became evident dispensing gasoline and kerosene was no longer profitable for the "Mom and Pop" stores in rural America. Vendors catered to the larger service stations and convenience stores where there was a demand for cheaper retail prices and an equally rapid turnover of sales. The smaller rural stores were forced to buy the gas they sold from one of the larger retail stores. The price they had to pay was just pennies below the retail prices being paid to those stores by the average consumer. Resale of this product afforded absolutely no profit for the small store owner. Subsequently, for Daddy and other merchants in the immediate area, gasoline sales diminished. The inside store purchases customers usually made while their gas was being pumped dropped dramatically when fewer cars stopped for gasoline.

Some of the customers realized Daddy was struggling with the onset of dwindling sales. One of the men suggested that he offer another product that would offset the loss of sales because of the gasoline crisis and encourage customers to stop and shop again. He began,

"Oris, why don't you start selling beer and wine? Most of the other stores around here are selling beer and they are getting more business coming in their stores."

Daddy replied,

"I don't want to deal with a bunch of drunks hanging around! Plus, there is no way Ruby will go along with beer and wine sales in this store."

A second man pointed out,

"You wouldn't have to deal with any drunks. When you buy your license to sell beer and wine, all you have to do is tell them you want off-premises license."

The first man added,

"Yeah, that's right. Whoever buys the 'stuff' will have to go somewhere else and drink it because they can't drink it on your property."

Daddy listened with interest. He thought,

"Maybe that's not such a bad idea. I've got to do something to bring in a little more money. Something's got to give or else I might as well shut the doors."

He remained somewhat reluctant to sell alcoholic beverages; yet, he didn't rule out the possibility of changing his mind. After all, he had been known to consume the beverage himself. However, he took every precaution to make sure Mother was never aware of his "habit."

Mother, on the other hand, was a firm believer that alcohol consumption was a sin. That belief, coupled with the blame she placed on alcohol consumption for the death of her brother, age 33, in an early morning car accident, caused her to condemn all alcohol beverages, no exception.

I awakened one night to the sounds of elevated voices coming from the direction of my parents' bedroom. Motivated by curiosity, I eased down the hallway and listened outside their door.

"That could not be my parents. No way. They, to my knowledge, never argued over anything."

Then, I heard Daddy exclaim,

"Ruby, be reasonable! People like beer and wine; and, they're going to buy it somewhere!"

Silence fell over the room. The he began to speak again,

"We've got to make some changes if we want to stay in business. If that means selling beer and wine, I don't see what harm there could be."

Apparently, Mother was giving him the silent treatment. The only voice coming from the bedroom continued to be Daddy's.

"Well, I've made up my mind! Tomorrow morning, I'm going to Raleigh and apply for the off-premise beer and wine permit so we can start selling them at the store."

Finally, Mother spoke.

"You do what you want to, Oris Gay!"

Whoa! That really grabbed my attention. She sounded angry. Guess she could become a little feisty with someone other than me when they met her disapproval.

"Go ahead! Sell your old beer!"

After a short pause, she continued,

"I promise you one thing. I will never sell one drop of that nasty stuff!"

And with that said, the conversation ended abruptly.

Daddy proceeded with his plans to include beer and wine sales in his store.

Mother remained uncompromising. She absolutely refused to sell alcoholic beverages. For those individuals who entered the store and tried to purchase these beverages, she stated,

"You will have to come around the counter and ring up your own purchase. Put your money in the cash register."

So adamant was she in her disdain over the situation, she ardently refused to allow her hands to touch any money received from those sales.

She even insisted that the customer reach under the sales counter, retrieve a paper bag to conceal their purchase, and then exit the premises. She would have no part of the sale; and, that was final!

Customers characterized her as a person with a sweet spirit, hospitable and a gentle disposition. She was respected by all who came to know her because of the way she carried herself. Because of this, they readily accepted her position on handling beer and wine sales.

Some of the regular customers found her "stubbornness" funny. Others shook their head and honored her requirements. One thing was for sure, no one dared argue with her about it!

Daddy may not have agreed with her decision; but, he respected her right to abstain. He never again mentioned alcohol sales or her refusal to compromise.

It was a win-win situation!

Chapter Twenty-Two

SERENITY INTERRUPTED

Outside the store window was a beautiful tree in vernal bloom. Sweet smells of spring were in the air. This Saturday, the 23rd day of April, 1949, was calm and serene affording all the comforts of a laid-back afternoon. Daddy had just returned to the store from driving Mother and me to my grandparents' house to spend the evening. Several of the men in the community, having finished their supper, had all gathered to listen to a baseball game being aired over the radio in the rear of the store. Apart from a somewhat heated dispute over some play in the game, this began as just another lulling and mundane day at the old country store.

The radio was blasting a game from Fenway Park being played by two arch-rival Major League baseball teams – New York Yankees and Boston Red Sox. The intense competition between these two teams generated loud outbursts of cheers or sneers among the men in the store. Legs outstretched and arms folded, when they were not ardently vocalizing their excitement over their favorite team scoring, these men sat relaxed on the long wooden bench immediately behind the old stove. So much depended on the outcome of this game, as well as the final games of the season. Only a few more games to be played and the winner of the American League would be determined and the opportunity to face the National League winner would be imminent. The 1949 World Series Championship banner hang in the not-so-distant future. The intensity of this realization ignited sparks of competitive speculation. Who among these sports-enthusiastic customers would be the one to correctly predict the outcome of this game?

Bottom of the ninth, two outs, and the pitcher hurled a fast ball. The umpire yelled,

"Strike three, you're out!"

The Boston Red Sox maintained the lead and defeated the New York Yankees by a final score of eleven to eight.

After the game finished, the usual argument ensued and the ongoing debate about players and their statistics began. Dorsey "Jack" Gay began and often ended these debates. After all, to this group, he represented baseball.

A few weeks prior to Jack's birth, his father, Floyd, and a friend attended a ballgame in Raleigh, N.C. where the Piedmont League was playing. A well-known shortstop by the name of Dorsey Daniel was playing. Jack's father was so impressed with the shortstop he promised his friend he would name his next son after that ballplayer. Floyd and his wife had a son; Floyd honored his promise and named him Dorsey Daniel "Jack" Gay.

Maybe it was instilled in Jack to live up to his namesake or maybe he just naturally loved the game of baseball. Either way he, too, became well known for his playing abilities and his knowledge of the game. Jack served his country in the U.S. Navy. After his discharge, he remained in Santiago and played professional baseball for the Santiago Padres. When an argument presented itself, he was always ready for the challenge.

"Think DiMaggio is going to win MVP this season?"

"There is no way he can out hit Williams! Granted, DiMaggio is on a good hitting streak; but, Ted Williams remains the best hitter of all. Nobody else can even come close to outhitting him."

"You know all there is to know about baseball. I'll give you that; but, you are wrong this time, my friend. This is going to be the year DiMaggio breaks the records and ends up being MVP. You just wait and see!"

The heated argument continued as the challenged man retorted,

"Hey, let's make this interesting. How about a little wager on who will be MVP, smart guy!"

Completely engrossed in their rousing conversation, the customers were oblivious to two young boys who, wearing masks and carrying a gun, had just entered the front door of the store.

"This is a stick-up," one of the young men anxiously yelled.

He pointed his small-caliber gun at Daddy and demanded,

"Open that cash register drawer and give me all your money!"

Daddy complied with the robber's demands, opened the cash register, and stepped back out of the way. The young boy holding the gun instructed his accompanist to retrieve the money from the cash register drawer. He then approached the area where the customers were still talking to each other.

"Lie face down, flat on the floor! Toss all the money in your pockets and your wallets to the side!"

The men remained transfixed on their baseball discussion and paid little notice to what was happening in the front of the store.

One of the men was predicting that in October the World Series would be won by the Yankees.

"The Yankees are going to be champions once again. I'll go you one even further, the Red Socks better enjoy today's victory because they'll be history by World Series time this year."

Rumbling disrupted as others expressed their point of view on the projected winner. (As fate would have it, on October 9, 1949, the New York Yankees did, in fact, win by defeating the Brooklyn Dodgers in game number five of the World Series. This was "their second defeat of the Dodgers in three years and the twelfth championship in team history."

Annoyed because he was unable to gain their attention, the robber fired a shot into the floor just inches adjacent to where the men were sitting.

"What the…" exclaimed McLean "Pete" Privette. His voice trailed off as he looked up and saw the man pointing a loaded gun in his direction.

The gunman became increasingly angry because his demands were not being taken seriously. To emphasize his point, he fired more shots into the floor.

"I said drop to the floor, now! Face down! Toss your money and your wallets on the floor where I can reach them!"

Exchanging looks of disbelief at one another, the men hesitated. Slowly they complied with the perpetrator's demands and dropped to the floor. Jack and Pete, the ones closest to the robber, immediately emptied their pockets, removed their money and their wallets, and tossed them across the floor. The perpetrator collected, in addition to the wallets, about twelve to fifteen dollars in cash from them.

Meanwhile, Russell Gay unlatched the pocket in the top of his bib-overalls, removed his wallet and slowly slipped it underneath the side of the potbellied stove.

In addition to his personal money, Haywood Raybon had a small pouch containing money for Beulah Church. When he realized both robbers had their backs turned, he carefully removed the bag from his pocket and threw it under the backside of the stove.

Amid the mass confusion that followed, Haywood managed to avoid being seen by them. He quietly and slowly backed out the door at the rear of the store. Once outside, he quickly fled the scene and hid behind the shrubbery surrounding the porch at our house behind the store.

His escape did not go entirely unnoticed. The young, twelve-year-old brother of the fifteen-year-old and eighteen-year-old robbers was waiting in their 1938 pickup truck parked outside. Once the young boy saw someone running out the back, he became frightened and started blowing the horn.

"Will, Gill, come on," he screamed.

Filled with panic, he kept blowing the truck horn and yelling.

"Hurry up! Somebody just ran across the backyard of the store. Let's get out of here!"

When his brothers still did not return, he screamed,

"He's gonna call the law, I know it! We need to go now! The law's gonna catch us for sure. Come on y'all and let's get the heck out of here!"

The older brothers ran out of the store and headed for their truck. Before they fled the scene, they fired shots in several directions outside. One bullet randomly penetrated the gas tank area of Russell's new 1949 Mercury. That was a big mistake! This latest act added "fire to the fury" once the already angry robbery victims exited the store.

Completely adamant over the audacity of those "young punks" who held them at gunpoint and robbed them, Daddy and Russel drove their trusty new Mercury and Hudson to the tanks out front and filled their cars with gas.

No stranger to high-speed driving, they were not afraid to drive wide open down the dirt roads and were confident those boys had no clue how to escape them. Determined to seek retribution for the injustice they had endured, they waited for Jack and Pete to ride with them.

Pete, who lived across the road from the store, ran to his house and grabbed his revolver. When he returned, Russell called out to him,

"Come on, get in. Roll the window down and hold your gun out."

Pete held his gun out the window and held on as Russell sped out of the store yard and down the bumpy dirt road.

"Try to shoot the tires out on their truck just as soon as we get close enough to them."

Jack, who lived two houses behind the store, ran home and retrieved his pistol. When he returned to the store, Daddy called to him,

"Grab a box of bullets off the shelf and keep that gun loaded. Keep your gun cocked and hold on."

Jack replied,

"We're going to show some boys what happens when they take money from the good old country folks at the county line. They're going to wish they had never seen this part of the country before."

Daddy, by this time, had that old Hudson in the wind. He glanced over at Jack and said,

"Keep shooting and don't stop until you run out of bullets and that's going to be a while."

Ten-year-old Aubrey Gay arrived at the store on his bike just as the cars sped off. He went into the store to see what was going on. Someone was on the phone calling the authorities. He listened as the man described the details of the robbery.

"Three boys escaped in a 1939 pickup truck and headed toward highway ninety-six. Our men are in pursuit and will try to catch them and hold them until the law gets there."

He paused a moment and listened to what a man who had just entered the store had to say.

"Tell the law they better get here. There's a crowd getting involved in the pursuit and they are all 'spitting' mad."

Aubrey grabbed his bike and rushed home to tell his parents. He and his dad, Leonard, got into their car, and went to the store. There was no one there so Leonard closed and locked down all the doors and windows and cut off the gas tanks. He and Aubrey proceeded to head to highway ninety-six and join in the chase.

Meanwhile, with a reckless speed reminiscent of their younger days of racing, Daddy and Russell "put the pedal to the metal" in their trusty Hudson and Mercury. Leaning out the window of the passenger side of each car, and with loaded gun in hand, both Jack and Pete were ready and eager to fire their weapons when they approached the rear of the boys' truck.

For miles around, sounds of roaring vehicles and gunshots firing could be heard. My grandfather, Ebbie Martin, hearing what he thought was gunfire, became concerned and walked outside to investigate. After a few minutes, he returned. He had a puzzled look on his face when he turned to talk to Mother and Grandma. I had an unexplained gnawing in my stomach and an uncomfortable sense of fear that something was terribly wrong. I questioned Grandpa's mysterious expression and he proceeded to explain.

"I've been trying to figure out what is going on. I heard what sounded like gunshots being fired. Ruby, it really sounded like they were coming from the direction of Oris' store. There are a lot of rumbling and roaring sounds coming from trucks. It sure sounds like the whole country is full of trucks flying up and down the road."

Mother telephoned the store. She was unable to get through because the phone line was busy. She again tried to get through, but to no avail. The third time she tried, the line was no longer busy. After several rings and no answer, she hung up the phone.

"Well, I guess Oris must be on his way to get us. The store must be closed because no one is answering the phone."

We were unaware, at the time, of all the "excitement" at the store and the countless number of vehicles engaged in hot pursuit throughout the encompassing area.

While we waited for the sound of Daddy's car to approach and reassure us of his safety, Uncle Edsel and his new bride, Carrie, returned home from a movie in Wake Forest.

My uncle hurried from his car, approached the kitchen, and spoke with uncanny excitement when he came through the door.

"When we crossed over 401, coming down ninety-six, we were passed by a fast-running pickup truck being chased by a whole line of cars and trucks. The men in the first cars were exchanging gunfire with the men in the truck. We had to drive in the ditch and they still almost hit our car when they passed by us. One of the cars in that chase looked just like Oris' Hudson. I believe it was him!"

Needless to say, this information created some very anxious moments for Mother and me.

"This can't be happening! Unreal. This is unbelievable. Tell me you are mistaken."

Mother tried to calm me down but her words left me with little reassurance. I could hear the panic in her voice and see the fear in her eyes as she spoke.

"Nothing like this ever happens around here. Your daddy is probably caught up in the traffic. He will be here anytime now and everything will be alright."

Meanwhile, the chase continued. Have you ever visited a pumpkin farm and tried to weave your way through one of the wheat-straw mazes, or gone to the fair and tried to find your way through countless rows of mirrors? If so, then you can imagine the predicament and sense of frustration those young robbers must have experienced. Pervading the unfamiliar and unpaved back-country roads, weaving in and out of Wake County into Franklin County and back again, they frantically attempted to elude their outraged chasers to no avail. No matter which road they traveled, the robbers soon learned every road led them back to the same area they had robbed. They were completely lost and found it impossible to elude that angry mob in relentless pursuit.

Word of the robbery and the ensuing chase quickly spread throughout the community. Soon the boys encountered more outraged citizens. These citizens, with shotguns visibly displayed in the back window of their trucks or on the front seat of their cars, joined in the pursuit.

Sixteen-year-old Franklin Barham was driving along highway ninety-six with his girlfriend and became caught up in the crossfire when the pursued truck passed them and bullets zoomed in every direction. One of Franklin's neighbors backed his vehicle into a driveway, grabbed his rifle and took aim at what he believed was the getaway car. He did not realize the vehicle at the end of his rifle scope belonged to Franklin and not the robbers. He assumed the pickup truck deliberately passed the car to block the getaway car. Therefore, he took aim; but, fortunately for Franklin and his date, he did not follow through and fire on the vehicle.

By that time, law officers arrived on the scene. The local citizens were aided by Wake County Deputy Massey, Zebulon Police Chief Hopkins, ABC Officer Perry, and Corporal Griffin and Patrolman Cash of the State Highway Patrol.

Deliberately remaining oblivious to the visibility of firearms on the seat or in the back window of the vehicles they stopped, officers enlisted the aid of several drivers to gain insight into the situation.

"Have you seen three young boys in a 1939 pickup truck?"

"Which way were they travelling?"

The officers followed the leads they obtained, and trying to keep this whole escapade under control, they continued on their way.

Their determination withering and facing impending exhaustion, the boys continued to elude their persistent followers. Multiple exchanges of gunfire were relentless. Speeding around a sharp curve on Mitchell Mill dirt road, they lost control of their truck and plowed into an embankment just a few yards from the bridge. Even as the vehicle chase ended, these boys were still unaware that their miles of driving had brought them back to only two miles from the store they robbed.

The sun faded and encroaching darkness surrounded. The terrified young men jumped from their truck and fled into the woods. Cars and trucks lined both sides of the road. It was virtually impossible to move past the rows of parked vehicles. Outraged men formed a mob-like gathering. Angry cries echoed throughout the crowd,

"Let's get them stinking rats! We'll make sure they don't ever rob anybody else."

From a far corner of the crowd, one voice rang out,

"I saw them run into the woods behind that house. Come on men, the fun is just beginning."

A couple of the officers stepped up with outstretched arms when the first group approached.

"Stop right there before this whole situation gets out of control. We have a good idea where they are hiding. There is no way they can escape now. Just let the officers do their job and bring this to a peaceful conclusion."

With the crowd contained, the officers, and a select few citizens who knew the area well, combed the woods in search of the fugitives.

Sometime later, they came upon three exhausted and fear-consumed young men. Sensing the onslaught of the infuriated crowd that had gathered and fearing oppression, the boys willingly surrendered to the authorities.

"Please arrest us or whatever you have to do. All we want is to get away from all those crazy people that have been following us," they pleaded.

The three young brothers surrendered without incident. They were taken into custody and placed in the officers' cars. The pursuit ended peacefully and the perpetrators were transported to jail to await trial.

The officers searched the get-away truck for evidence of the robbery. They found $54.31 in cash, two wallets, two masks and one 32 pistol.

The brothers confessed to this robbery. An article written in a local paper stated,

"They also admitted being responsible for a similar hold up in Franklin County, a week earlier, where they confiscated between $25 and $50. In addition, they confessed to a hold-up near Chase City, Virginia, a week prior to the Franklin County incident. In Chase City, they took $80 and the 32-caliber pistol used in the subsequent robberies."

The two younger boys were turned over to juvenile authorities for prosecution. The eighteen-year-old was charged with armed robbery and sentenced to prison. Years later, we learned he died in prison before serving his full incarceration term.

For the next few weeks, conversation around the potbellied stove no longer focused on crops planted, fish caught, or the numerous typical topics discussed on a regular basis. Instead, the events of April 23, 1949 became the topic of interest. Of course, with each repeated account of the incident came a different presentation of flair. The dramatic effect depended on who recited the events that transpired on that memorable day.

One of the customers, Pete Privette, who was among those in the center of all the action, recounted an interesting previously unknown fact about his in-store encounter with one of the robbers. Pete wore a white shirt to the store that afternoon. During the robbery, he was ordered to lay face down on the floor. Only after the whole ordeal was over and he had returned to his home did he examine his shirt. Even when he complied with the robber's demands and lay stretched out, face down on the store floor, he never got a dirty spot on that white shirt.

Years passed and the intense excitement of that Saturday afternoon encounter diminished. One thing remained constant. Security took on a different meaning for those loyal patrons who gathered together to gossip and swap truths and yarns. The serenity of this friendly environment had definitely been interrupted!

Jack Gay

Teen-Agers Held In Theft

Three teen-aged brothers, caught shortly after allegedly pulling a bandit-style hold-up of a store near Youngsville on Saturday night, also have admitted robberies in Franklin County and Virginia, Wake County officers said yesterday.

William Lockett Womack, Jr., 18, oldest of the trio, was bound over to Wake Superior Court under $5,000 bond following a hearing before Magistrate H. A. Bland. Gilbert Matthess Womack, 15, and Elvin Medlin Womack, 12, have been turned over to juvenile authorities, Deputy Sheriff G. C. Massey reported. Their home is at Oxford, Route 2, the deputy said.

According to Deputy Massey, the two older boys, armed with a pistol and wearing masks, entered the store of O. B. Gay near Youngsville and informed the occupants that a stick-up was in order. When the men in the store hesitated, one of the boys fired a shot into the floor, the officer said.

The patrons then were told to lie down on the floor and throw out their pocketbooks, which they did. The youthful stick-up men collected $40 from the cash register, $8 and a pocketbook from Dorsey D. Gay, and $4 and a wallet from McLain Privette, and made their getaway in a 1938 pickup truck, which the younger boy apparently had been waiting in, Deputy Massey related.

After a chase, the boys wrecked the car on a road a short distance from the store and took to the woods, he said. They were rounded up early Sunday morning.

In the truck, Massey said, officers found $54.31, two pocketbooks, a .32 automatic pistol, and two masks.

The brothers confessed to the robbery and admitted similar hold-ups in Franklin County on April 16 and near Chase City in Virginia on April 9, the officer said. About $80 or $90 and a .32 pistol were taken in the Virginia robbery and between $25 and $50 in the Franklin theft, he said. Officers from the two places have asked that the boys be held for them following their trial in Wake County.

William Womack, Jr., has been charged with armed robbery and was being held in Wake County jail in lieu of $5,000 bond yesterday. Deputy Massey said that the 15-year-old boy might be bound over to Superior Court also.

Aiding Deputy Massey on the case were Zebulon Police Chief W. B. Hopkins, Constable S. T. Blackley, ABC Officer D. H. Perry and Cpl. C. D. Griffin and Patrolman J. M. Cash of the State Highway Patrol.

Chapter Twenty-Three

DON'T MESS WITH HIM

Regardless of the steady increase of large and expanded grocery and variety stores available, one thing remained unchanged. The old country store was still a favorite pastime for the locals.

Slowly, throughout America, factories emerged and provided work for those who chose to stop farming and travel back and forth to the city for employment. As a result, there were fewer men having leisure time to hang out at the country store.

A new generation of patrons emerged. Boys who had accompanied their dads and granddads became the new generation of regulars at the store. Most visits to the store were brief. People had little time for gathering around and talking.

Jerry Mitchell, who for years came with his dad, Durwood, remained a daily patron. He aspired to someday own his own country store; a dream he realized a few years after the closing of OB Gay's store. Stores, by this time, were referred to as "convenience" stores.

Jerry Mitchell

On a bitter-cold Tuesday afternoon, November 2, 1976, Jerry stopped by the store prior to departing for his nightshift job at a correctional institute in Butner, N.C. He purchased a small pack of cigars, removed one, struck a match, and puffed away. He paused only briefly to take a sip of his favorite ice-cold Coca Cola.

Another local, Rudolph Baker, entered the store and the two friends exchanged greetings. Conversations between these two men were often argumentative. Usually, to the delight of their audience, they were extremely comical.

Rudolph spoke with a fast-paced, slightly high-pitched voice. Often, in his haste, he ran his words together. Jerry, contrastingly, had a more subdued tone with a cleft-palate enunciation. One would have to listen intently to understand what they were saying. Some patrons, especially those visiting from out-of-state, paused in astonishment and amusement as they attempted to interpret the conversation. Entertainment at the old country store materialized in various forms of sights and sounds.

Rudolph Baker

While these two men delved deeply in the day's subject matter, the occasional clinging of the cash register could be heard as customers entered, made their purchases, and exited the building. This was a typical weekday at the store. As fate would have it, the chain of events that followed was anything but typical.

Around 4:50 PM, two young men entered the store. Daddy did not recognize either of them. The weather outside was freezing cold; thus, the fact that both men were attired in long, heavy black overcoats was no cause for alarm. Snugly clinging to their overcoats, neither man wore a hat nor a cap on his head. In retrospect, this may have been an indication the two young men had made a last-minute decision to dress in such manner.

Both men walked around in the store and contemplated their intended purchase. One man turned and walked over to the checkout counter where Daddy was standing. With a voice barely above a whisper, he asked,

"Do you have any potato chips?"

Daddy gave him a puzzled look and then replied,

"Yes, they are on the display rack at the far end of the candy case over there."

The man grabbed a bag of chips, handed Daddy his money, glanced over at his friend, and promptly walked out the front door.

In the meantime, the second man continued to look around. First, he stopped at the candy case and stooped down to view the variety of goods for sale. He slowly stood up and glanced around the store. Afterwards, he walked up and down along the long row of wall shelves stocked with merchandise. He paused long enough to lift and replace various can goods and packaged boxes.

His suspicious behavior continued for several minutes. Daddy was not necessarily uneasy as he watched this man. However, he increasingly became agitated with the man's indecisiveness and inquired,

"Can I help you find something?"

Without saying a word, the man turned around and removed a twelve-gauge, sawed-off shotgun from underneath his overcoat. He placed the gun on the checkout counter and pointed it straight at Daddy's face.

Characteristically, Daddy was a man slow to anger; and at the age of sixty-six, he was even slower to move. On this particular occasion however, he impulsively grabbed the gun barrel, caught the would-be perpetrator off guard, and pulled him over the counter. Both men fell backwards with the gunman landing on Daddy.

Thank the Lord, the two customers, Jerry and Rudolph, had remained in the store. They rushed over to assist. Jerry utilized his guard-training skills from his Butler job and jumped on the attacker and pulled him off Daddy. Rudolph removed his trusty switchblade from his pocket and joined in the scuffle. Thanks to the quick response from these two men, the robbery attempt was thwarted and Daddy's life, once again, was spared.

Once Jerry and Rudolph successfully subdued the perpetrator, they sat him down on the floor in front of the upright drink machine across from the counter. Here they held him captive until law authorities arrived on the scene.

Composure restored, Daddy regained his stability. He grew angrier over the realization of what had just happened. Subsequently, he withdrew his twenty-two-caliber pistol from underneath the back side of the checkout counter. Glaring at the young man, and now with a steady hand, he aimed his gun directly at the captive's head. The captive circled his arms around his knees while he sat motionless directly in front of Daddy.

With a glaring look that could penetrate a stone wall, Daddy blurted out,

"Go ahead, move! I dare you. If you so much as blink your eyes, it will be the last move you ever make. I guarantee that!"

The young, twenty-year-old perpetrator had two accomplices. One left the store after purchasing potato chips and the other waited outside in an early model blue car. Both men fled the scene once they realized their friend was involved in a large commotion inside the store.

Rudolph rushed out the front door and ran across the road to Sophia's Beauty Shop. He watched as the perpetrators' car rapidly sped out-of-sight toward Zebulon. He explained to Sophia the incident that had just transpired at the store and asked her to please phone the authorities. Then, he returned to the store to assist in the captivity of the gunman.

Sophia immediately telephoned the Zebulon Police Department,

"O. B. Gay's Store has just been robbed. Two customers are holding one man inside at gunpoint."

The officer inquired,

"How many men are involved?"

Sophia replied,

"There were three of them but two have already gotten away. You really need to send someone out here right now! Word is spreading and a lot of cars are starting to fill the parking lot."

Even though this incident was well out of the jurisdiction of the Zebulon Police Department they recognized the urgency. They were very familiar with this rural area and deemed it necessary to respond promptly and attempt to prevent what was destined to become an uncontrolled situation. Since they could reach the crime scene faster, the Zebulon police responded and placed the attempted robbery suspect in protective custody. They handcuffed him, placed him in the back seat of their car, and held him until the county authorities arrived.

Outside, an angry crowd gathered around the police car and began shouting threats and demands,

"Let us at him! Somebody grab a rope. Let's string him up! Show him a little county-line justice like the old days around here."

The police officer anticipating the possibility of a riot, rolled his window down about an inch and exclaimed,

"Let the law handle this. The county authorities are on the way. We are going to keep him in our car until they get here."

Three angry, red-faced men, with their fists clenched, banged on the window of the police car,

"We don't need any law! We are the law! That no good scoundrel came here for excitement? We will give him plenty excitement, all he can handle and more! Turn him loose! Let us take care of him."

At that point, several more men came forward. In a mob-like movement, they surrounded the car. They placed their hands above the windows and forcefully rocked the vehicle back and forth.

A roar of sirens penetrated the air. Flashing red lights illuminated the evening sky as the Wake County Sheriff Department's cars approached the scene. While a couple of deputies contained the crowd, another deputy removed the suspect from the police car. He secured the man in the sheriff's car and transported him to county jail to await trial.

Back in the store, Daddy noticed Jerry had tied a cloth around his arm. Blood had seeped through the cloth and turned it bright red. He walked over to his friend and asked,

"Jerry, what in the world happened to your arm?"

Jerry responded,

"Damn if I know. Somebody either bit me or cut me with a knife during the scuffle. I'm left with a deep-cut gash. I tried to stop the gushing blood with my pocket handkerchief as a tourniquet. From the looks of this wet, red cloth, I don't think I did such a good job. I need to get some medical attention now!"

One of the law officers overheard the conversation, assessed the situation, and immediately retrieved his phone,

"I need an ambulance at O.B. Gay's store. In an attempted robbery on the premises, one man sustained deep stabbing wounds from a knife. He has lost a lot of blood and needs emergency assistance!"

Jerry was transported to Zebulon-Wendell Hospital. He received several stiches in his arm and an injection to prevent spread of infection. He was released and instructed not to go to his night job but to go home and rest. Though he was frustrated over the restriction, he complied with the doctor's orders for calm relaxation and sleep.

Rudolph received a "busted lip." Fortunately, he did not require any stitches nor additional medical attention. Daddy, because of the quick action of his two friends, only suffered minor scratches and a wounded pride.

Later, in an interview with a reporter from "The Zebulon Record," Daddy recounted the events of the day.

"I realize now that I could have been killed when I grabbed that gun; but, at the time, it seemed like the only thing to do. I don't think I had time to be scared, it all happened so fast."

He credited his friends, Jerry and Rudolph, for their quick action in pulling the perpetrator off and holding him captive.

"If they hadn't been here; well, no telling what might have happened."

A few weeks later, a reporter from "The Raleigh Times" came to the store and interviewed Daddy.

"I can't get about too fast, but I can handle myself," Daddy confided to the reporter.

Rapidly taking notes on his writing pad, the reporter inquired,

"How did you feel when you were staring at a single-barreled shotgun being pointed at you?"

Daddy continued by saying his pistol was in reach, but that shotgun barrel only a foot away scared him.

"I threw up my right arm and knocked the gun away and grabbed it with my left."

"I jerked him and the gun all over the counter."

The reporter, whether intentionally or unintentionally, presented an article filled with sensationalism. He painted a misguided picture of an elderly store proprietor who single-handed managed to thwart an armed robbery. Additionally, the reporter, while writing about the foiled robbery attempt, entitled his article,

"Don't Mess With O.B. Gay."

Although we understood the reporter's enthusiasm in his journalistic effort to capitalize the moment, we remained apprehensive over the title to which he attached. For many months afterwards, we agonized over the possibility that some would-be-robber, trying to make a name for himself, would show up. In an attempt to gain notoriety by becoming the person who successfully "messed with O.B. Gay," he might pull off another robbery and possibly a murder in the process. This, in a sense, was not unlike the old west when a fast draw invited more challengers.

Thankfully, time passed and the news article was not challenged.

Robber taken
O.B. Gay thwarts armed theft

A community store owner thwarted an armed robbery attempt last Tues., Nov. 2. At approximately 4:50 p.m., two young black men entered the store of O.B. Gay, on Rt. 3, 3 miles north of Hopkins. The first man bought a bag of potato chips, and when Gay asked the second if he needed some help, he withdrew a 12 guage shotgun from underneath an overcoat, and pointed it at Gay.

Gay, who is 66, impulsively grabbed the gun, pulling the would be robber over the counter with it.

Two friends of Gay, Jerry Mitchell and Rudolph Baker, who were in the store at the time, rushed over to assist him. The three men held the man, who was later identified as Calvin Caldwell, until Zebulon police arrived on the scene.

Caldwell's two accomplices, one who was waiting outside in an early model blue car, fled when Gay jumped Caldwell.

Caldwell, 20, of 3008 Snowberry Drive Raleigh, was held at the Zebulon jail until Wake County law officials arrived. He was later transferred to Raleigh. A warrant has been signed against him for attempted armed robbery.

Gay's friend, Jerry Mitchell was taken to Zebulon-Wendell Hospital for stitches in his arm from a cut or bite received in the scuffle. Baker received a busted lip, and Gay suffered some scratches.

"I realize now I could have been easily killed when I grabbed that gun, but at the time it seemed the only thing to do," said O.B. Gay. "I don't think I had time to be scared, it all happened so fast."

Gay credits his friends Mitchell and Baker for successfully holding the robber.

"If they hadn't been here, well, no telling what might have happened," Gay added.

Since he opened his store located on S.R. 2303 in 1933, he has now been held up twice.

"That first time in 1949, three young men came in with masks, and there were six of us in the store. They made us all lie down on the floor, and took three pocketbooks and some wallets from us," Gay recalled. "I caught them too. I chased them for ten miles before I caught them and turned them over to the sheriff."

Thwarts bandit
Gay, shown outside his Hopkins community store, successfully halted a robbery last week.

Robbery attempt foiled
Don't mess with O.B. Gay

Don't mess with O.B. Gay.

"I can't get about too fast, but I can handle myself," confides Gay, 66, the owner of a country store in East Wake.

Gay proved that Tuesday when a man pulled a single barrel shotgun out from under his coat and pointed it at him.

"I knew I had to do something right then," the storekeeper said this morning.

Gay's pistol was in reach, but that shotgun barrel a foot away scared him. "I threw up my right arm and knocked the gun away and grabbed it with my left."

"I jerked him and the gun all over the counter," and then he and several customers wrestled the man to the floor and held a pistol on him until the police arrived.

One of the customers had to have some stitches to sew up a cut or a bite on the arm, another busted his lip in the scuffle and Gay suffered a few scratches.

A warrant has since been signed against Calvin Caldwell, 20, of 3008 Snowberry Drive, Raleigh, for attempted armed robbery on Gay's store located near Zebulon on S.R. 2303.

Gay was robbed once before which convinced him not to let a robber have his way.

That was in March 1949, and those guys didn't get away either. Gay said he chased them ten miles in his car before catching them. He turned them over to the sheriff too.

Chapter Twenty-Four

INNOCENCE OF A CHILD

During the summer of 1982, Daddy, age seventy-two and requiring the assistance of a walker to move around, loaded his fishing gear and drink cooler in the back of his Chevrolet pickup truck. At last he managed to escape the encompassing walls of the store and relax on the bank of his family's ten-acre pond. He turned over the duties of the store to Mother and ventured out on his peaceful afternoon fishing endeavor.

There were no customers in the store and Mother was enjoying the quietness. She had just ended another pleasant conversation with her young friend Butch Baker. After he left the store, she rested on the seat in front of the window located behind the sales counter. A gentle breeze from the small tree outside the window embraced her. She heard a car motor running out front and looked out to see an elderly couple pull up to the gas tank.

The lady stepped out of the car and walked around the outside of the store. She entered through the back door and slowly edged her way to where Mother was now standing. The lady had never been in the store before, so naturally, she looked around as she approached the counter.

"Do you have a bathroom that I might use?"

Mother replied,

"I'm sorry, we do not have any indoor plumbing or bathroom facility in our store."

The lady thanked Mother and exited through the front door where she joined her husband who was attempting to pump gas into his car. The gas pump was outdated. Capacity to be controlled from within the store was not an option. Additionally, the pump was troublesome to operate because of the speed with which it ran. Several customers often referred to the lightning speed at the gas tank.

"That's the fastest pump I've ever seen. If you ain't careful, you will overfill your car in a hurry. Gas will be all over you and the ground," stated the elderly gentleman.

The rear door of the couple's car opened and their two little grandchildren jumped out and ran into the store.

"Can you please help Papa pump some gas? He don't know how to get that pump to work. It just won't work!"

Mother willingly walked outside and assisted the man. She explained to him that many people had the same problem trying to operate that old pump. It had the reputation of being the fastest pump around.

A few minutes later, the grandchildren returned to the car. The man thanked Mother for her assistance, paid her for the gas and slowly departed.

About that time, Peddler King, drove up and walked back into the store with Mother. She went around the counter to ring up the gas sale and place the money in the cash register. The cash register, like the outside pumps, was outdated. It was manually-operated and nickel-plated unlike the newer electric models that were circulating in nearby stores. She attempted to press the keys down,

"What's wrong with this cash register? The keys won't move. They are all jammed tight together and I can't get them to unlock the cash drawer."

Peddler realized her frustration, offered his assistance, and opened the cash-register drawer, much to the relief of Mother. She placed the money in the drawer and closed it. With a sigh, she proceeded to relax on the bench behind the stove.

As Mother moved slowly along the checkout counter, she suddenly paused. She noticed the bank bag kept on a small shelf beneath the backside of the counter was missing. The bag contained money received from the previous day's sales. The money was scheduled to be deposited in the bank the next business day.

She stooped down and searched under the counter.

"What happened to the bank bag I had under this counter?"

Peddler joined in her search and asked,

"Mrs. Ruby, are you sure you put that bag under the counter? Maybe Oris took it with him when he left."

Mother replied,

"I know it was there this morning because I counted the money and filled out the deposit slip to be carried to the bank. Oris would not have taken it to the pond with him, no way!"

She and Peddler looked around the floor, underneath the counter, and in the office desk at the rear of the store. Overwhelmed and unnerved, Mother questioned Peddler,

"You don't think those little innocent children could have taken the money, do you?"

He replied,

"Well, Mrs. Ruby, it shore looks like they did. They must've been just after the money. Look there under the counter. The pistol is still on the shelf. Maybe the gun scared them."

Mother became extremely anxious and exclaimed,

"What should I do? Who do I call? I can't let them get away with this!"

She continued,

"What is Oris going to say when I tell him two little 'youngins' took all the money we had for the bank from yesterday's sales. There was also money in the bag that we use for making change in the cash register for our customers."

She rubbed her hands together as she paced.

"I can't believe I was so gullible. I allowed those old folks to deceive me. And those innocent looking little children with their sweet and smiling faces. The nerve of them! All the time, they were here with the intent to trick a woman, alone, and rob her. Just look what they are teaching their little ones to do. What is this world coming to? This beats all!"

Peddler finally managed to calm Mother down and they telephoned the authorities. Once again, for a third time, a Zebulon police officer was dispatched to the scene assist the county deputy who was in route.

According to the officer, Zebulon and surrounding areas had experienced several similar get away robberies over the previous few weeks. Persons fitting the same physical description, and driving the same make and model car, had been perpetrators in those incidents. Unable to catch these thieves or prove anything against them, the law was prevented from prosecuting them, even though the authorities were almost positive they knew who the family members were.

Ruby back at Cash register with Pete Privette

Found within a few miles from the store was the bank bag the children confiscated. Of course, the bag was now empty and the evidence to prosecute was embedded in the grass along the roadside. Thus, the criminals were never apprehended and brought to justice.

Mother was content just to drop the whole matter. She considered herself blessed because no bodily harm had been inflicted on her during this unfortunate incident. Daddy and I concurred and were very thankful for her safety and that her life had been spared.

While recapping these events, I learned from C.A Lloyd that his dad's store, The Red Bird, was also subjected to robbery attempts. C.A recounted how a couple of months prior to daddy purchasing the store from Lonnie Lloyd one such attempt occurred.

Once a year, the North Carolina State Fair came to Raleigh. The performances and their acts usually arrived one week before the public could attend the fair. During the 1930s-1950s, a group of gypsies travelled with the fair. Quite often, they were mischievous, often rowdy, and sometimes left the fairground and wandered into the rural areas of N.C. On more than one occasion, they chose a small country store and engaged in a robbery. More than one year, they showed up at The Red Bird. Lonnie Lloyd's sons, Thraudy and Cody were just before leaving the store at the end of the day when a band of gypsies burst into the store. They were armed with a shotgun and demanded the sales money the Lloyd brothers were carrying. In an added scare-tactic, they paused, turned around and blasted a shot into one of the store panels. The Lloyds made no attempt to confront them. Rather, they remained calm and handed over the money. Once they were sure the intruders had exited the premises, they turned the key to lock the door and made their way to safety. Whew!

Chapter Twenty-Five

MONDAY MORNING MYSTERY

January 1983 began and continued to be an extreme wintery-cold month. Daddy, now seventy-two years old, had suffered a stroke which left him with a slight speech impediment and difficulty in moving around. Additionally, Mother's health had steadily declined.

To help them realize their lifelong dream of remaining in the store business for fifty consecutive years, I opened my bookkeeping and tax business in a closed off area in the rear of the store. By doing this, I assisted them in the operation of the store until they could reach their desired goal.

Amid the frigid coldness of that January 1983, serenity at the country store was once again interrupted. Unlike the previous invasions, the events that took place were not just a one-time incident. Rather, they were once-a-weekend repeated occurrences that continued for several weeks.

Days of operation for this store, Monday through Saturday, remained constant from 1933 through 1983. Daddy and Mother ignored the insistence of some patrons for them to capitalize on the big cities' "Blue Laws" and benefit from sales to customers who were not allowed to shop in town on Sunday.

After we filled the drink boxes with all the various sodas, made sure all the shelves were stocked and merchandise moved forward to the edge, we locked the doors and exited the building. When we returned in the morning, all we did to become operational was fire up the old potbellied stove, sit back and await the arrival of the customers that day. We were not open on Sundays; therefore, there was no reason for us to enter the store at all on that day. Occasionally, we would open the doors long enough for Uncle Edsel and his family to get a soda and snack and share a quick visit as they were on their way from church to Mr. Rogers' house.

Shivering from the bitter cold outside, one Monday morning we entered the store and noticed something was missing from the shelves on top of the drink box. There was a two-tiered glass shelf which rested on the elongated Coca Cola drink box. These shelves housed fresh nabs purchased from Lance Company. Nabs were stacked neatly in rows with the "square" ones on the top shelf and the "round" ones on the bottom shelf.

When we left the store on Saturday night, both shelves were filled with fresh nabs. On this Monday morning, there were no nabs on the bottom shelf.

Daddy turned to me.

"Are you sure you put the round nabs on the shelf before we closed Saturday night?"

I adamantly replied,

"I am positive. I stacked two full boxes of round nabs on that shelf before we left the store."

Puzzled, we looked around the store in search of the missing boxes of nabs that needed to be put on the display counter. We encountered discarded empty boxes from which both square and round nabs had been placed earlier on the shelves.

Daddy shrugged the matter off,

"Well, whoever took them must have been hungry. We'll just have to tell the Lance man to bring us extra nabs this week."

Unfortunately, this was not a one-time incident. For the next few weeks, we opened the front door of the store on Monday and faced a bottom shelf devoid of any round nabs. Obviously, the thief entered on Sunday while the store was closed.

To solve this puzzle, we entered the store right after church on the following Sunday. To our dismay, both the round and the square nabs rested on the shelves and untouched. Indeed, this was turning into a mystery.

Monday morning, we faced the same scenario. No round nabs on the bottom shelf. We looked outside the store for tire tracks on Monday mornings and under the store shelter for any evidence of intruders. Nothing was found.

Then, after an overnight freeze wave, we entered the store and heard loud popping noises resounding from the side room. This room housed drinks and other merchandise which was moved into the main section of the store on an as-needed basis.

We opened the door and found, because of the extreme ice-cold weather conditions, countless filled drink bottles had burst. Glass and debris was all over the floor.

We cleaned the mess, picked up the wooden drink cases and stacked them in a corner. Upon moving one drink case, we discovered a large hole in the floor beneath the case. The hole was about eight inches long and five inches wide and appeared to be a rat's burrow. These burrows are usually found beside a structure. In this case the structure was the stacks of drink crates on a thick-hardwood floor. Rats use these burrows to flee from something or someone they consider to be a threat.

To our dismay, the outer edges of the hole were surrounded by layers of empty round nab wrappers. Why he chose the rounds nabs as opposed to the square nabs was still uncertain. Normally the vision of these rats is known to be very poor. Consequently, we assumed he employed another sensory for his selective choice of nab shape. Ultimately, we concluded the round nabs were chosen because they were situated on the bottom shelf and therefore more accessible to the "thief."

Daddy exclaimed,

"Looks like one big, healthy wharf rat found a new way to satisfy his hunger urges this winter."

His conclusion seemed feasible in view of the fact rats are omnivorous animals and will eat almost anything. They especially love peanut butter and thus these nabs became a delicacy for this particular rodent.

We enlisted the aid of our neighbor, W.B. Privette, to capture the four-legged intruder. W.B. brought one of his large animal traps over and put a fresh cut of hoop cheese on it. After placing the "bait" to lure the rat, he set the spring release and placed the trap near the empty hole.

Late the next night, we readied the store for the following day's operation. We checked the locks on all the doors, approached the side door, and placed the pipe lock in its slot. After hearing a loud snap coming from the side room, we opened the door and discovered one whopping big Rattus Norvegicus, commonly referred to as a wharf rat. He was a nasty brown rodent with coarse hair, a tail as long as his body, and appeared to be almost two feet long. He was definitely larger than the average house mouse. We stared at him and he, in his trapped position, stared back at us with his big green eyes. We closed the door, again replaced the lock, and proceeded to exit the building for the night.

The next morning, Daddy again enlisted the assistance of W.B. to remove and discard the culprit. Once we were convinced we no longer had a resident in the side room, we covered the rat's secret entrance.

Alas, the Monday morning mystery solved, serenity was once again restored and extra round nab purchases were no longer necessary.

The remaining months of 1983, which constituted the final year O. B. Gay's store remained in operation, were fortunately not interrupted by invasion of thieves.

Unfortunately, two of their fellow convenience-store operators in the area met with tragedy as a result of their stores being robbed. Both times, the perpetrators were local young people who often had patronized their stores and had been treated cordially by the owners. On January 31, 1981, Roy Argo "Mitt" Perry, age 71, was robbed and killed by a young man who lived a few houses from his store. Again, on June 23, 1989, Billy K. Hopkins, one day after his 75th birthday, was robbed and murdered in his store by a neighborhood youth. The cruelness and senselessness of these murders resounded throughout the community and surrounding areas as friends and neighbors mourned the deaths of two outstanding and well-liked men. After Mitt's death, we were increasingly anxious to complete the next two years of our store business, prayerfully, without incident.

By the Grace of God, Daddy and Mother overcame their life-threatening and sometimes mysterious encounters. Ultimately, they realized their desired goal and celebrated fifty years operation in their country store haven.

Not unlike a successful marriage, these two proprietors, together, faced the good times and the bad times. They conquered the unknown and strengthened their eagerness and determination to persevere. The thieves only managed to remove material things. What Daddy and Mother perceived to be important in life remained constant throughout their journey.

Chapter Twenty-Six

HIS JOURNEY ENDS

December 31, 1983 arrived and the fifty-year journey came to a pretty uneventful end. Aside from a reporter from the local newspaper who came out to take pictures and do a feature article on the closing moments of this historical event, only a few well-wishers stopped in to say good-bye.

All the merchandise had been removed from the store shelves. Some of it was taken to the house. Some was given to loyal customers. Some of the advertising signs and merchandise displays were sold to collectors. Several filled trash cans awaited transport to the dump.

Empty shelves were covered with stains and dusty residue after products were removed. The barren floors held scratches from sliding equipment over the years and splatters from spittoon-aimers' poor aim. Faint smells of dust mixed with chemicals and lingering tobacco smoke from cigars and cigarettes presented an odd mixture commonly associated with the country store gathering place.

Daddy methodically placed the long, oak rail across the double wooden doors at the back of the store and secured it in the deep-bolted holders. More than a thousand times over the years he had exercised this ritual; however, this time was different. Alas, it would be the final security assurance for these doors.

He walked to the door leading into the side room. There he placed an eighteen-inch galvanized pipe into a hole that had been drilled at a forty-five-degree angle through the left side of the door connecting into a sturdy-built door frame.

Slowly, he turned and walked to the opposite side of the store. He went behind the checkout counter where the late afternoon sun was shining through a side window. He lifted the bottom window, pulled the solid-shutter door by its latch, and placed a bolt through the slot. Another lock secure, he let the inside window down and exited the counter area.

He paused, propped on his walker and gazed at the surroundings. His eyes focused on the high beams, the empty shelves and showcases, and the heavy-trodden floor. He took a few steps, paused again and placed his hand on top of the old potbellied stove. In his moment of silence, he looked fondly at the stove and thought,

"Goodbye old friend. I will surely miss you."

He walked to the front door, stopped, and looked around. The entire room was filled with silence as he reached his hand into his pocket and removed the keys. He slowly exited the door, positioned his walker, turned around, and leaned forward to face the door. With a shaky hand, he placed the key in the lock and snapped it shut. He paused to look at the faded blue screen door with its Merita Bread advertisement. Then, ever-so-cautiously, he released the door and listened as it slammed shut on five decades of dedicated service.

That was it!

Finally, he had attained his desired goal: he claimed his golden anniversary as a country-store proprietor of his own business.

Though he experienced a hollow, sinking feeling in his stomach, he managed to display a proud smile on his face.

With a forlorn look, Russell stood underneath the store shelter and waited for his brother to join him. The two men walked in silence around the corner of the building. They paused only briefly to breathe a deep sigh, neither of them able to openly express their inner feelings. (Men just didn't publicly display emotion in those days!)

Daddy and Russell were the only remaining siblings in their family. They were accustomed to being together several days a week. They would miss the many hours shared just relaxing and talking. This would be their last "visit" because men were comfortable coming to the store; but, when it came to visiting in the home that was "for the women folks."

An underlying sadness evoked when the two neared the rear of the building. Russell paused at his pickup truck and placed his store merchandise and mementos on the seat. I grabbed my camera and coaxed them into posing for a photograph as they stood together on that memorable day, December 31, 1983. Daddy watched sadly as Russell drove away. Unfortunately, that was the last time they were together. Russell passed away just three months later on March 18, 1984.

Mother joined Daddy and they walked together down the path to their house. This day had brought an end to fifty years of conducting a country store business dedicated to providing needed supplies to the people of their community. To the proprietors of this mom n' pop business, Oris and Ruby Gay, operating this store and assisting their neighbors had been a "labor of love."

What a privilege afforded me to have grown up in this country store environment surrounded by our rural area farm. My entire existence revolved around family and friends who enriched my life, molded my values, strengthened my faith, and filled me with a sense of pride. If ever I viewed my childhood as mundane, the reminiscences unfolded in this tribute to my parents and their beloved country store definitely disputed that claim. To that end, I will forever be thankful for those "country store collectibles" of my youth!

Oris & Ruby behind the counter on the last store-open day

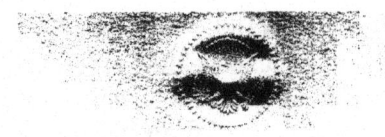

THE WHITE HOUSE

WASHINGTON

December 22, 1983

Dear Mr. Gay:

I was pleased to learn of your many years as a merchant. You can take great pride in your work. Stories like yours are encouraging and inspiring, for it is hardworking individuals like you who make up the backbone of this nation.

Nancy joins me in sending our warm best wishes for every future happiness and success.

Sincerely,

Ronald Reagan

Mr. O. B. Gay
Route 3, Box 256-AA
Zebulon, North Carolina 27597

Brenda, Ruby & Oris Gay

Made in the USA
Columbia, SC
19 November 2017